Fans Called Him "Turkey,"
I Called Him Dad

D1526819

Fans Called Him "Turkey," I Called Him Dad

A Daughter Remembers
Baseball Hall of Famer
Norman Thomas Stearnes

ROSILYN STEARNES-BROWN

Foreword by GARY GILLETTE

McFarland & Company, Inc., Publishers
Jefferson, North Carolina

ISBN (print) 978-1-4766-8891-6
ISBN (ebook) 978-1-4766-4697-8

LIBRARY OF CONGRESS AND BRITISH LIBRARY
CATALOGUING DATA ARE AVAILABLE

Library of Congress Control Number 2022049980

On the cover: *inset* Norman "Turkey" Stearnes in his
Chicago American Giants uniform (1932); Stearnes holding daughter Joyce
with wife Nettie Mae, daughter Rosilyn (the author, standing on bumper)
and the author's uncle John Foote in the parking lot of the Eastern Market (1949)

———

Printed in the United States of America

*McFarland & Company, Inc., Publishers
Box 611, Jefferson, North Carolina 28640
www.mcfarlandpub.com*

*To the memory of my dad, Norman Thomas
"Turkey" Stearnes; his fellow Negro Leaguers,
who played not for fame but for the love of the
game; and my mom, Nettie Stearnes, who tried
for 20 years to get Dad into the Hall of Fame
and lived to see her efforts take flight. As she
said at his induction, he was "a star born to
play baseball, one who belongs with Stars."*

Acknowledgments

I would like to acknowledge and thank the following people for their love, patience, dedication and cooperation in providing me with materials that I needed for the factual and emotional content of these memoirs:

Joyce Stearnes Thompson—my sister
Joe Lapointe—sportswriter/journalist
John Collier—sportswriter/journalist/photo provider
Gary Ashwill—provider of Dad's most current statistics
Syrennia Hanshaw—cousin
Phyllis McArthur—aunt
Gary Mitchem—senior editor, McFarland

Special heartfelt thanks to Gary Gillette for the foreword and for the love that he has shown to my family in carrying on Dad's legacy; Jim Petersen, who helped in formatting the photos; and Sandra Burgess, who worked tirelessly with me as my local editor to prepare my manuscript for the publisher. Their work was indispensable.

Contents

Contents

Foreword
by Gary Gillette

It is a rare privilege for a commoner to be welcomed by a royal family, yet that is how I feel about my experiences with the family of Norman "Turkey" Stearnes over the years.

Along with the families of Motown stars from the 1950s and 1960s, the Stearneses are a branch of Detroit's royal family. When they are present, everyone looks to them. When they enter a room, everyone stops talking for a minute and then points out their presence. As a non-native Detroiter and as a white person, I have found their graciousness and warmth toward me both unexpected and humbling.

Rosilyn Stearnes-Brown and her sister, Joyce Stearnes Thompson, have treated me like family, and I am very grateful for the time and affection they have bestowed upon me as well as for their intense interest in their father's legacy.

The Stearnes family's participation in baseball events in Detroit is always a highlight of any gathering. Rosilyn and Joyce, along with their departed and beloved mother, Nettie, have graced many gatherings, including the Detroit Tigers' annual Negro Leagues Tribute Weekends, local Society for American Baseball Research (SABR) meetings, and several Negro Leagues–themed conferences and symposiums.

The SABR Southern Michigan Chapter (formed by a recent merger of the Detroit and West Michigan chapters) has enjoyed Rosilyn's and Joyce's attendance at many meetings. Nettie's, Rosilyn's, and Joyce's participation at the 2014 Jerry Malloy Negro Leagues

Conference in Detroit was a signal event, especially because they were joined by several younger members of their family.

As Rosilyn notes in this book, baseball, music, and family have been constants in their lives, and what more felicitous combination is there for us mortals?

The public appearances of Turkey Stearnes' widow and the Stearnes sisters have been especially important in cementing the memory of their Hall of Fame father because Turkey Stearnes was a man of few words himself, even when given the opportunity to talk about his stellar career.

Norman Thomas Stearnes lived for 39 years after he retired from the Major Negro Leagues before the 1941 season, and for 34 years after he last played ball professionally for the Toledo Cubs of the United States League in 1945.

Regrettably, no film of Stearnes as a player is known to have survived—if, that is, any film of his career ever existed. (Videotape and video recorders had not yet been invented in the first half of the 20th century.) The only audio of Turkey Stearnes we have is a precious snippet recorded on a cassette in 1979 shortly before his death.

Preserving and promoting the career of Turkey Stearnes is vitally important because Stearnes was one of the greatest power hitters in baseball history. Moreover, for multiple reasons, his stellar career was vastly underrated until recently—and, even with its newfound prominence, I believe his accomplishments remain yet underappreciated.

Nettie Stearnes lived a long and good life, passing in 2014 at the age of 96. Unlike her soulmate, she was fortunate to have lived long enough to see her husband's enshrinement in the National Baseball Hall of Fame in Cooperstown in 2000—due in no small part to her hard work to ensure her husband's legacy.

The induction ceremony in rural Cooperstown in July 2000 was bittersweet, though, as everyone knew it had come 21 years too late. If it had come during Turkey Stearnes' lifetime, we would have video of the great ballplayer to cherish, audio of his most likely humble and short acceptance speech, and hundreds of photos of Stearnes sharing the dais with Carlton Fisk, Tony Perez, and Sparky Anderson.

Fortunately for baseball fans everywhere, but especially for Detroiters and fans of the Negro Leagues, Rosilyn and Joyce have accepted the mantle of promoting their father's career. Now they have been joined by Rosilyn's niece, the articulate and passionate Vanessa Ivy Rose.

The greatest African American ballplayer to wear a Detroit uniform for most of his career is not yet universally known even in the town where he loyally played, worked, and raised a family with his adored Nettie. Evidence of that too prevalent ignorance can be found in Stearnes' embarrassingly belated induction into the Michigan Sports Hall of Fame in 2007.

The career and life of "Turkey" Stearnes demonstrated a steadfastness and a faith that is rarely seen today, an old-fashioned commitment to work and family that transcends the impermanent relationships of too much of American life in the 21st century.

Before Rosilyn penned her memoirs, people outside of Detroit could only know her father through the handful of print interviews published during his retirement, through the recollections of his contemporaries—both teammates and opponents—and through his extensive statistical record. Even those telltale stats, however, were not widely available until the past decade.

It is not disrespectful in any way to local hero Willie Horton or to the underrated Lou Whitaker—who should be in the Hall of Fame in Cooperstown alongside his White teammate Alan Trammell—to say that, without any doubt, "Turkey" Stearnes was the greatest black ballplayer to spend most of his career in Detroit.

Our cultural dependence on video and audio recordings as foundational to our memories makes it harder to envision the greatness of "Turkey" Stearnes. Nevertheless, thinking of Stearnes as a left-handed Willie Mays or port-sided Hank Aaron can help.

According to the authoritative statistics from Seamheads.com, now published on Baseball-Reference.com as well, Stearnes played at 6-foot-1 and 185 pounds. James A. Riley's magisterial *Biographical Encyclopedia of the Negro Baseball Leagues* listed Stearnes as 6-foot-0 and 175 pounds avoirdupois. Either way, the silent and slender slugger packed an enormous wallop in his bat.

Foreword by Gary Gillette

According to the *ESPN Baseball Encyclopedia*, the only reference work to have ever published the range of playing weights for ballplayers during their Major League Baseball careers, Aaron was listed at 6-foot-0 and 170–180 pounds. Mays was recorded as 5-foot-11 and weighed 170–185 pounds. Both batted right-handed; both are in the top ranks of the National Pastime's greatest players and greatest home run hitters.

So is "Turkey" Stearnes, who stands shoulder to shoulder alongside immortal sluggers like Mays, Aaron, and Josh Gibson in baseball's Valhalla.

Gary Gillette is the founder and chair of the Friends of Historic Hamtramck Stadium, one of only five remaining major Negro Leagues home ballparks. In 2020, he successfully petitioned the City of Hamtramck to name the historic field after Norman "Turkey" Stearnes. Gillette is writing a new history of the Detroit Stars and the Negro Leagues in Detroit, to be published in 2023. He is a 2021 recipient of the Society for American Baseball Research's prestigious Tweed Webb Lifetime Achievement Award, bestowed by SABR's Negro Leagues Committee.

Preface

I have an untold story to tell. My memoirs are about a man, very close to my heart, who came from humble beginnings and became known to people worldwide as a baseball superstar. He had the reputation of a quiet and reserved individual, but deep in his character were the powerhouse qualities that drove him to greatness. In these memoirs, he will be brought to life and remembered not only as a great ballplayer but also as a man, a husband, a grandfather, a friend and, most important of all, *Dad*.

My story began when Dad married Mom and they decided to have a family. Born to this union were two daughters. I am the eldest daughter, born on September 7, 1946, four months after they were married. I was blessed to know my father up close and personal for 33 memorable years. As I look back, it has seemed like a lifetime.

Throughout his baseball career, countless stories were told about his prowess, but to this day not much is known or said about his personal life and his family. He had two loves: baseball and family, and although I missed his Negro Leagues career, I can certainly speak with firsthand experience about the life he made with us.

Fans Called Him "Turkey," I Called Him Dad seemed fitting as the title for two reasons:

1. Fans knew him by his nickname, "Turkey."
2. He was a fantastic dad and my best friend.

When Dad put his foot down, something about him made you want to listen and to obey. I always felt as though I was going to miss

---

something if I didn't; other people felt the same way. Dad commanded attention in a way hard to describe. When he was on the field, he put on a show. People came from all over to see him run at record-breaking speed, make catches in the outfield that seemed impossible and hit prodigious home runs with unexplainable consistency.

It has been said that "you can't judge a book by its cover." This was so true about Dad. When he would take his stance at home plate, he looked as though he couldn't hit a fly. But once the ball crossed home plate—surprise! All doubt was gone. He left everyone in awe. His bat did the talking.

Regrettably, Dad's baseball career started and ended before my sister and I were born, but we heard the stories, both in our younger years and later, as adults. To fill in the blanks, I read articles and books about Dad and the Negro Leagues. I learn things about his playing days every now and again, some of them from baseball historians who, like Gary Gillette, continue to research and publish on the Negro Leagues.

Many times over the years I had considered writing about Dad from my own point of view but couldn't seem to get my memoirs off the ground. Then a professional editor and fellow member of my church asked, "With all that information about your dad, why don't you write a memoir? If you do, I will help with the editing." So, here we are.

Before my sister and I were born, Dad and Mom came through some trying times: World War I, World War II, the Spanish Flu pandemic, the Great Depression and racial discrimination. Through it all, they endured and excelled. Dad became a professional ballplayer, then completed high school, then worked at Ford Motor Company for nearly three full decades. Mom graduated from college and became a public-school teacher.

After I was born in 1946 and my sister, Joyce, was born in 1947, a new journey began. I couldn't have asked for a better childhood. Dad was a man of integrity and moral fortitude. He and Mom were married for 33 years, and their disagreements were exceedingly rare. Dad's commitment to Mom and his family was above reproach. I never heard him complain or gossip, and he was my confidant.

When I would hear Dad and his best friend, Satchel Paige, talking about their baseball days and how they weren't allowed to play in the major leagues because of the color of their skin, they neither complained nor expressed any bitterness. They took it in stride.

Dad had the same attitude while he was working in the foundry at Ford Motor Company. I watched him go to work every day like clockwork for 27 years. He was always on time and never willingly missed a day. This was despite the horrific conditions in the foundry, where the heat was tremendous and the noise deafening. Dad had to have the strength of a bull to work under those conditions, but he didn't complain.

Some of my most cherished moments with Dad were what I called our "father-daughter talks." All girls need a father like Dad. No matter what my situation was, I could rely on Dad's wisdom to make me feel better. I would sit on his lap with my head on his shoulder, and the comfort of his arms would let me know that he would be there for me no matter what. Dad was the same source of wisdom and comfort for his grandchildren, and the feelings were mutual. We were Daddy's children, and he was our confidant.

Education was important to Dad and Mom. I hope these memoirs not only inform people about Dad and the Negro Leagues but also show how he and his teammates lived their lives to the fullest. Future generations of young men and boys will see that Dad set a good example for them to follow on and off the field.

During my own career as an educator in the Detroit Public Schools, I discovered that the students and most of their parents knew not much about the white major leagues and nothing about the Negro Leagues and their players. They were hyped up about basketball and football. I hope that as they read these memoirs, they recognize that while men like my dad endured many of the struggles that we face today, including racial discrimination, they rose above the obstacles and excelled in a profession they loved. Dad was so great because he loved what he did. He didn't let anything get in his way.

At Comerica Park in 2007, after the unveiling of the plaque honoring my dad, one of my students asked me, "Ms. Brown, you mean to tell me that your dad played with a lot of other black ballplayers before Jackie Robinson?" I said, "Yes, he did. There were a lot of black ballplayers. They had their own leagues. They weren't allowed to play in the major leagues because they were black. When you get back to school, look up Negro Leagues ballplayers and you'll see what I'm talking about. You'll see my dad, too." He said, "Wow, Ms. Brown. I thought Jackie Robinson was the first black man to play baseball. Wow! I'm glad I came. You're famous, Ms. Brown." I said, "No, I'm not famous. Dad is." That was an educational moment for that little guy. Moments like that have made me realize that Dad's story needs to be told.

Outside of our family, Dad is being recognized during this centennial anniversary of the Negro Leagues as one of the greatest baseball players who ever played the game. To me, Dad was Dad, and he will always be the greatest.

Prologue

"Turkey was a man of great stature. He was tall, dark and hand-some, well dressed and very devoted. He was kind, quiet, honest, car-ing, strong, gifted and most of all loving. He had all the qualities that parents try to instill in their children. He never said an unkind word about anyone, and he loved baseball. We both did. It was his world, and he talked about it; he was one of the greatest baseball players to play the game. However, he wasn't concerned about being in the lime-light, so the thought of giving an acceptance speech probably would not have appealed to him.

"We were destined to meet and were married in Detroit, Michi-gan. Born to us were two daughters, Rosilyn and Joyce. Both are pro-fessional singers. Rosilyn is a music teacher, while Joyce is a teacher of the deaf and hard of hearing. We have five grandchildren and nine great grandchildren.

"After he retired from the Ford Motor Company in 1964, his daily routine consisted of waking up early, riding the bus down-town, taking long walks, and sitting in the barber shop [on Linwood] talking to his friends about baseball. He would ride the bus to Tiger Stadium and sit in the bleachers at all of the Detroit Tigers' home games. You could always tell when they were losing because he would arrive home early before the game was finished. Turkey and I spent many hours talking about the many home runs, triples, doubles and singles that he hit and how you couldn't play in the Negro Leagues if your batting average was below .300. He said that his power came from God and that his strength was in his arms and legs. He lived

---

and breathed two things, baseball and his children, and he had a high batting average in both."

Remarks by Mom at the induction ceremony of Dad into the National Baseball Hall of Fame, July 23, 2000.

I

A Legend Is Born

Life for my dad began on May 8, 1901, in Nashville, Tennessee, in the county of Davidson. His parents, Will and Mary Everett Stearnes, also were born in Nashville. They named him Norman Thomas Stearnes. The nickname "Turkey" came later during his baseball days. Will and Mary had four children, three boys and a girl. Dad was either the eldest or the second eldest. He was born before his brother Bennie and his sister, Louella, but one of the mysteries about Dad's family is his other brother. We found out that the mystery brother lived in Chicago, but there wasn't much talk about him, and we never met him face to face. In those days, when babies were born, they were delivered by midwives. Depending on the circumstances, births then weren't reported as accurately and as often as they should have been. The accuracy of the reports was totally up to the midwives. Dad's family was fortunate because the births in his family were accurate and on file.

Dad's family grew up during a time when the United States was in economic and social distress. They survived the Spanish Flu pandemic, the Great Depression and two world wars. The distress was especially true for black people. They weren't afforded the same opportunities that other ethnic groups had. As in most black families at that time, they were economically and spiritually challenged. In other words, they were poor in every sense of the word with little hope for achieving success. In spite of these crises, they relied on the old saying, "Tough times don't last, but tough people do." They turned their seemingly hopeless situations into opportunities.

Fans Called Him "Turkey," I Called Him Dad

Dad's parents died before we were born, so my sister and I never got a chance to meet them. We were told that Dad's father was a full-blooded Cherokee Indian, which is why Dad had the high cheekbones and reddish dark complexion. Most people say that Dad was dark skinned, but I say that he was a reddish dark. I think I'm right. We knew his sister, Louella, and one of his brothers, Bennie. Bennie and Louella were a key part of our family. We saw them often, but we never met or knew his older brother. I always wondered why. To this day I don't remember hearing any talk about his older brother or his family. I also don't remember why his older brother was never around or why no one thought to include him in being with the family. All I remember is that he lived somewhere in Chicago. I was a kid then, so I had many other things to think about. Now I have begun to realize how important it is to know family history and will try to make amends for my negligence. History, especially family history, is important.

Dad and his siblings attended Pearl High School in Nashville. They could not afford to go to college. They had to work to help support the family. In those days, children had a great deal of respect for their parents and other adults and had a deep commitment to their family. Family and education were synonymous. They were morally and spiritually connected.

When Dad was a teenager, he started playing baseball on the school team. He started as a pitcher. His coaches soon realized the tremendous talent he had. He was an all-around skillful player and exceptional in speed and hitting. His coaches suggested that he try out for the professional Black teams. This would afford him better opportunities financially and would enable him to experience travel around the country, which he couldn't do with a local job.

While Dad was still in high school, his father died; he felt compelled to help provide support for his family. So Dad quit school at the age of 15, tried out for one of the teams in the National Negro Leagues, and the rest is history. His decision to pursue a career in baseball was more lucrative than any of the other local jobs. His family supported him as best they could, but they had to accept getting whatever jobs were available.

Even though Dad had to delay his education in his teenage years to help support his family after his father died, he was determined to get his high school diploma. He completed his high school education and graduated at the age of 21.

Everything about Dad was unique from his base running, fielding, batting stance and the way he lived. Dad wasn't a drinker, didn't stay out late at night, didn't hang out in bars, didn't use profanity and couldn't care less what everyone else was doing. He would drink beer, but that's it. When he was playing ball, his teammates would party and hang out but couldn't get Dad to do the same. After a game, Dad would pack up his equipment, including his bat, and go home. He encouraged the young men on the team to do the same. One of his young roommates, Ronald Teasley, said that Dad would explain the rules and make sure that he followed them. Dad's emphasis was

Dad and his Monarchs teammates of 1934 standing by their struggle buggy in Denver. From left: Newt Allen, T.J. Young, Turkey Stearnes, Eddie Dwight, Dink Mothell and Bullet Rogan.

on education and being a success. No foolishness. One of his cardinal rules was that you should go to bed early and not participate in anything that would prevent you from meeting your obligations as a ballplayer.

During his baseball days, Dad had a reputation for being a sharp dresser. His good friend Satchel Paige and other teammates said that Dad was always well dressed. One of my favorite photos of Dad and five of his teammates is a picture taken while they were in Denver, Colorado. They looked sharp as tacks and were leaning against a car in their Sunday best. Great ballplayers, great dressers.

Nicknames

Nicknames were a part of Dad's life while he was playing ball and in his personal life. In our family, he gave Joyce and me nicknames. He called me Pretty Girl, and he called my sister Bugsy Bunny. I asked Dad where he got the nicknames from, and he said, "Well, I call you Pretty Girl because I like the popular song with the same name. It reminds me of you. I call Joyce Bugsy Bunny because she talks as much as Bugs Bunny in the cartoons." When Dad told me that, I fell out laughing. Dad laughed, too. He had a great sense of humor. He was quiet and reserved, but he could tell a joke when he wanted to.

He and his fellow ballplayers all had nicknames. These names were representations of their personalities, interests and the way that they played. There seems to be some discrepancy about how Dad got his nickname, "Turkey." There are interesting stories about how he got that name. Some say it was because of his awkward stance at bat; some say it was because of the way he flapped his arms when he was running; some claim that Dad said it was because of his potbelly. Dad and my maternal uncle, Ted Radcliffe, who was another Negro Leagues ballplayer, said it was because of his speed. Not many people know this, but turkeys can reach speeds of up to 25 miles an hour. That's why they're so hard to catch when they're not in a group. It's easier to catch them in a group. I tend to believe what my dad and my uncle said because not only did I hear it firsthand from them but also from other people who saw my dad play.

Satchel Paige, who was one of the greatest pitchers of all time and one of Dad's closest friends, said that Dad was fast. So did Cool Papa Bell, another player who was just as fast or even faster than Dad. Just to set the record straight, it makes more sense to say that Dad got his nickname because of his speed. That came straight from the horse's mouth.

My uncle Ted Radcliffe was called "Double Duty." A sportswriter was at one of the games where my uncle was playing in Chicago, and it turned out to be a doubleheader. In the first game, my uncle was the pitcher. In the second game, he was the hind catcher. The sportswriter exclaimed, "Hey, he's doing double duty." Ever since then, everyone called him Double Duty.

Felicity at Its Best

There's an old saying, "When life serves you lemons, make lemonade." That's indicative of the attitude my dad and the other Negro Leagues ballplayers had. I can honestly say that Dad wasn't bitter about not making it to the major leagues. It wasn't important enough to him. If asked, he would just shrug his shoulders and say, "White people in the United States weren't ready for Negro ballplayers. We were too good for them." He said, "It was a sign of the times." What a lot of people don't know is that the Negro Leaguers traveled around the world, and Dad said they were treated better in other countries than they were treated here. Sad but true.

Dad said that in order to play on one of the Negro Leagues teams, you had to bat at least .300 and play at least two positions. Many of them played more than two positions. When Negro Leaguers played the major league ballplayers, they would play positions that they had never played before and the major league teams still could not beat them. The games that the major leaguers won the Negro Leaguers let them win. This was so the interleague games would continue and so the Negro Leaguers wouldn't have to worry about suffering repercussions for embarrassing the major league players. Dad said Ty Cobb refused to play them. Ty Cobb was quoted as saying, "I'm not going to let those niggers beat me."

Dad played centerfield and first base; he also could pitch. He was an all-around skillful player. He could hit, field and steal bases. Statistics verify this fact. So will anyone, players and fans, who saw my dad play. Regrettably, my sister and I were born after Dad had retired from playing, but we know about his speed because Dad walked every day as part of his daily routine and did so at a fast pace. We had difficulty keeping up with him even when he became older. Most men his age had difficulty keeping up with him.

Dad told me that he was able to keep his average as high as it was (.300 or better) because he was a switch hitter, which meant that he could bat both right-handed and left-handed. When he faced a right-handed pitcher, he would bat left-handed. When he faced a left-handed pitcher, he would bat right-handed. He was equally good with both hands, another extraordinary feat.

When people would ask Dad if he kept count of how many home runs he hit, his response would always be "No, because if it didn't win a game, it didn't count." That's how humble Dad was. Statistics meant nothing to him. It was all about winning the game.

Carrying on the legacy of the Negro Leagues ballplayers and spreading the word about these exceptional men is a way of sharing lessons learned that can't be taught. They managed to be exceptional players and to pursue their dreams despite dangerous and degrading circumstances that were a part of their lives. In my opinion, based upon what I've seen, read and heard, my dad was the greatest baseball player of all time. Something to think about, isn't it? If you can say that about your dad, welcome to the club.

We don't have all the statistics concerning the Negro Leagues games because some of the records were destroyed and can't be found. There were black-owned printing companies that published Negro Leagues statistics. However, when the Negro National League got up and running and word got out about how good these players were, the

Klu Klux Klan would set the printing companies on fire to destroy the records. To save the records, these printers reacted by keeping them in other people's homes. This way, the printers were the only ones who would know where the records were being kept, and the individuals who kept them wouldn't say anything. Some people may have those records now or may have discarded them without realizing their historical value. It's sad to think how racism can have such a negative impact on the legacy and history of ethnic groups in this country. We all can learn from each other. We should embrace our differences and celebrate our talents so this world will be a better place.

The Negro Leagues ballplayers were extraordinary men with extraordinary talent. Yet because of the color of their skin, they didn't have an opportunity to play in the major leagues. Did that stop them from playing? *No!* They formed a league of their own and called it the Negro National League and made history. Imagine having to pile nine men into a 1920 Packard and then travel hundreds of miles to a baseball game because you had to travel in numbers to keep from getting lynched by a group of white men who didn't like black people, especially successful black people. Imagine, during this trip, not being able to go to the first bathroom you came to after a long drive for fear of it being a "For Whites Only" bathroom. Or imagine not having enough food to last for the whole trip and not being able to eat at any of the restaurants along the way because the restaurants were "For Whites Only."

Despite the callous and inhumane way they were treated, and all the obstacles placed in their way, they were able to overcome and still pursue their dreams of being professional ballplayers. I always say that they were able to make their mark in history because they played for the love of the game.

If Dad had not been inducted into the Baseball Hall of Fame, we never would have known just how great a ballplayer he was or about the other guys he played with, including my uncle Double Duty Radcliffe. These were real men. Men today could learn a lot from them. When my dad and other Negro Leagues players realized how difficult it was going to be to get into the major leagues and saw what Jackie

Robinson went through, they resigned themselves to getting other jobs and careers. They were all in their 40s or 50s, and most of them had families to support. They were forced to retire from playing ball and to look for other job opportunities.

Dad wasn't a quitter. Education was important to him, and he realized that it could lead to a career beyond baseball. While still a ballplayer, he went back to school and received his high school diploma at the age of 21. Under the same circumstances, and with what was happening in this country at the time, that was an extraordinary accomplishment. Most people would have just given up and let bygones be bygones. Dad wasn't like that. He was determined to set an example not only for his fellow teammates but also for the next generation and his family.

During the off-season while Dad was still a ballplayer, he worked for Briggs Manufacturing Company in Detroit, a maker of automobile bodies. The owner of the company was Walter O. Briggs, Sr., who also owned the Detroit Tigers baseball team. Briggs would not allow Negro players on his baseball team. He was quoted as saying, "No jigs with Briggs." Consequently, the Tigers were one of the last major league teams to become integrated. After gaining experience in the automotive industry while at Briggs Manufacturing Company, Dad went to work at Ford Motor Company's River Rouge plant.

II

A Celebratory Beginning
After Baseball

Dad met the love of his life when he was 44 years old. He had retired from baseball and moved to Detroit when my Aunt Baby Doll introduced him to her sister Nettie Mae McArthur. My aunt and my mom were both living in Detroit. Baby Doll's real name was Velma McArthur Husband, but everyone called her Baby Doll or Doll Baby. Nettie Mae was to become my mom. She was 17 years younger than Dad.

Her mother, Olga McArthur, wasn't in favor of encouraging Dad and Mom's relationship. Because of Dad's age and occupation, she didn't want them to develop a marital relationship. My grandmother, whom we called Mother, had several concerns. First, there was the age difference between Mom and Dad. Second, Dad had only a high-school education while Mom already had graduated from college. In addition, Mother McArthur was what we called "color-struck." Dad was dark-skinned, and she wasn't too happy about his looks. She liked fair-skinned, handsome men with good hair, and that's what she wanted for my mom.

As fate would have it, Mom and Dad were married despite her objections after a whirlwind courtship. Their marriage was consummated on Dad's birthday, May 8, 1946. I think Mom chose that date to make it easy for him to remember their anniversary. After their marriage, they bought a home on the east side of Detroit and Dad's life was never the same after that.

Mom was born in Sheperdsville, Alabama, on St. Patrick's Day,

March 17, 1918. Her parents were Olga (née Radcliffe) and Cazzie Clinton McArthur. The McArthur children comprised five boys and seven girls. Mom was the fourth oldest child. Her family, like Dad's, also experienced hard times. They were very poor. Their family size only complicated the situation.

At that time, women were not encouraged to practice birth control, and my grandmother didn't believe in it anyway. She believed that children are a blessing from God. My mom and her siblings would joke that their father was having so many kids because he wanted to keep my grandmother barefoot and pregnant so he could keep tabs on her. My grandmother was having children so fast that some of the siblings were barely nine months apart. My sister and I would have a good laugh when Mom would tell us these stories. Mom said they didn't think it was funny at the time but later could laugh about it. Despite their poverty and the economic conditions at the time, they were a close-knit family and worked hard to live a better life and they succeeded in doing just that. Grandfather McArthur died before Joyce and I were born, but we had some good times with Mother. She was the one who started us singing and playing the piano.

My mom was an honors student throughout school. Before moving to Detroit and meeting my dad, she had earned a bachelor's degree in English from Miles College in Fairfield, Alabama. After graduation, Mom became a teacher in the public-school system in Alabama. Mom continued teaching after she and two of her sisters moved to Detroit. She taught in public and private school systems, at church and in theological seminaries. Teaching was her passion, so she would do it whether paid or not.

I think one of the reasons Dad was so attracted to Mom was not only for her looks (if I do say so myself, Mom was a pretty lady), but also because she was an educator. An affinity for education was something that Mom and Dad had in common because they both loved children. He wanted us to be the best that we could be, and education was the key.

Mom and Dad had a lot of things in common, and one of the important ones was their love of the outdoors. Mom said before they were married, and when Dad had some free time, they would drive around Belle Isle and enjoy the attractions, the animals and the calmness of the water. Mom said they would get as close to the water as they could and sit and watch the boats go by and just relax. Mom said Belle Isle was better than any of the other parks she had ever been to, and Dad agreed. But she remembered one incident that made them a little cautious about going to Belle Isle, especially when Dad was driving.

She said they had been on one of their outings to Belle Isle on a Sunday afternoon and were on their way home, driving down Jefferson, when a police officer pulled up behind them and flashed his lights. She said Dad pulled over to the side of the curb and turned off the ignition. When the police officer came to the driver's side of the car, Dad rolled the window down and said, "What's the problem, officer?" The officer walked around to the other side of the car where Mom was sitting and looked at her. Mom said she got the impression, from the way he was looking at her, that he thought she was a white woman. That's why he pulled Dad over. When he got closer, he could see that she wasn't; plus, when Mom asked the officer, "Why did you pull my husband over?" she said he didn't respond. She said he knew for sure that she wasn't a white lady because she didn't speak like one.

So the officer walked back around to the driver's side of the car and asked Dad for his driver's license. Holding the license in his hand, he walked around to the front of the car and asked Dad to turn his lights on. Mom said by this time she was very irritated and wanted to know what he was doing. He had no reason for stopping Dad. Then the police officer said, "Turn your lights on." Dad turned his lights on. Mom said she didn't understand what that had to do with anything because it was broad daylight outside and Dad wouldn't have been driving with his lights on. She said, "You didn't have any reason to pull him over!" Dad gave her a look and shook his head. He didn't want her to say anything but she did anyway. Mom has never been afraid to speak her mind. The police officer ignored her and said to Dad, "Okay, turn your lights off."

Then he walked back to the police car and sat for about 10 minutes. Mom said after he came back to Dad's car and handed him a ticket, Dad asked, "Why did you give me a ticket?" The officer said, "For dim lights. Get them fixed." Dad put the ticket in his pocket and drove off. Mom said she was furious and asked Dad, "Why didn't you say something? How could you get a ticket for dim lights in the daytime? You know why he pulled us over!" Mom fussed all the way home.

A few days later Mom asked Dad what he did with the ticket. He said, "I paid it. I didn't want any trouble." He knew that if Mom had gotten a hold of the ticket, she wouldn't have let him pay it. She wanted him to go to court and stand his ground. Dad didn't like confrontation, so he did the next best thing: he paid it. Mom was aggressive and outspoken; Dad wasn't.

Mom and Dad had opposite personalities in several respects. Dad was unpretentious and let his actions speak for him. He was a quiet and rather private man but not antisocial. One thing I can say about my dad is that he never had a bad word to say about anyone. Dad chose his words carefully. He reminded me of a popular television commercial aired many years ago about a stock conglomerate, EF Hutton. The ad would say, "When EF Hutton talks, people listen." I felt the same way about Dad. When Dad spoke, you had to listen. I learned, in later years, that I could tell him anything. He wasn't judgmental and wouldn't repeat what you said.

Both Mom and Dad were sharp physically and mentally, loved their family and were morally sound. They made a handsome couple as well. Photographs of them when they were young proved Mom was a pretty lady and Dad was a handsome man.

It wasn't long after Mom and Dad married that their family grew with the birth of two darling girls. I was born Rosilyn Norma Stearnes, named Norma after Dad, on September 7, 1946. My sister, Joyce, was born a little more than a year later. After her marriage, she changed her name to Joyce Stearnes Thompson. Joyce acts like she's the oldest, but she's not. I allow her to do that just to keep the peace. I look more like Mom, and Joyce looks more like Dad, but you can see the family resemblance in both of us. A few people have said that Joyce and I look like twins. I strongly disagree. "Beauty is in the eyes of the beholder."

II. A Celebratory Beginning After Baseball

When I was born, my mom and my dad had a small disagreement as to what my name should be. Dad wanted a namesake (even though I was a girl), so he wanted to call me Norman. Mom said, "I'm not naming my daughter Norman. That's a boy's name. Let's compromise. Her first name will be Rosilyn and her middle name Norma." Dad said, "Okay, agreed." There was no disagreement about my sister's name. Dad just wanted to make sure that his firstborn was named after him. Although he had two daughters, no sons, I never once heard him say that he regretted not having any sons. I think that that was because the two of us were a handful. Sometimes my mom would say, "Turk, good thing God only gave us these two 'cause if I had any more just like them, I'd have to drown them." Of course, she was kidding.

When Mom first became pregnant, she and Dad decided that she would defer her teaching career and become a dedicated housewife and mother. That's what she did. Dad got no arguments from Mom. Mom wasn't teaching at school, but she was doing a very good job with us at home. She tutored Joyce and me as well as other children in our extended family and neighborhood. She officially resumed her teaching career after we became teenagers in high school.

Dad and Mom worked together to ensure that we excelled in school and would accept nothing less. The majority of the time we complied. Joyce was a talker, so she would get poor citizenship grades, and, of course, there were consequences. Dad did the scolding. Mom did the spanking. I didn't want to suffer the consequences, so I was the quiet one. I got that from Dad, plus I knew Mom was heavy-handed. They took turns signing our report cards, and together they attended parent-teacher conferences and our performances at school.

Being in a family with three women proved to be a challenge for my dad that he readily accepted. I always wanted a brother and asked my mom on many occasions why we didn't have a brother. She said that she and my father had tried to have a son, but her pregnancies were always difficult. After two miscarriages and a stillbirth she couldn't have any more children. She said that she was Dad's second wife. They never really talked about his first wife. That was another family mystery that will remain a mystery. All we know about Dad's first wife is her name. We know that only because one of the baseball researchers from the Society for American Baseball Research (SABR) found out who she was and found the wedding license. They were married; that's all we know.

One of Mom's favorite pastimes was telling us stories about Dad during our early years when we were too young to remember them. She loved telling stories. For every situation, she had a story. One of my favorites is about Mom and Dad taking me to the pediatrician for regular checkups when I was a baby. Dad would drive us to the doctor's office and let us off at the front door before parking the car. Mom would check in, find us seats and save one for Dad. When Dad would come in and sit next to us, everyone in the office would give us strange looks and talk quietly among themselves. Mom would get a kick out of that because she knew what they were thinking.

Dad was considered dark-skinned (actually, he was more of a reddish color). Mom and I were considered fair-skinned, and both of us had green eyes. The people in the doctor's office thought Mom and I were white, and Dad was black. They couldn't figure out what was going on. They were probably thinking, "Why is this white woman with this black man?" Mom said later that she didn't help the situation any. She would sit me in Dad's lap and lay her head on his shoulder. No one dared say anything; they were too polite. But if looks could have killed, Mom and Dad would have been dead a thousand times over. When it was time to leave and Dad pulled up in front of the door, all eyes were on us. Mom turned around with me in her arms, waved goodbye and we left. Mom and Dad would chuckle all the way home.

Another of Mom's stories that was indicative of the times was about a baby contest sponsored by the *Detroit Free Press* in 1949. Mom mentioned the contest to Dad, and he told her to go for it. He said, "Put both of my girls in the contest. That way we'll have a better chance of winning. It's a good chance that we will be the only family that has two contestants from the same family." Mom said, "Turk, you're right. Let's do it." So they did. I was three years old and my sister was two.

II. A Celebratory Beginning After Baseball

At the contest, Mom held Joyce and me by the hand and tried to get to the registration table while Dad parked the car. Dad was taking too long, so she decided to register us and to save him a seat in the auditorium because time was running out. She didn't want us to miss the contest. As Mom was hurrying us along, I was busy looking elsewhere and not really paying attention to her. Mom said, "Roz, keep up. We've got to hurry." And wouldn't you know it? When she said that, I tried to walk a little faster, tripped and fell. Neither of us had seen spilled coffee on the floor, and I fell onto the spill and ended up with a big stain on my dress. While Mom was trying to figure out what to do, lo and behold, here came Dad. Mom picked me up, brushed me off and told Dad to take me to the bathroom or someplace where he could get the stain off of my dress. Meanwhile, Mom would register my sister. That way at least one of us would be in the contest. Dad picked me up and headed towards the bathroom. Mom got to the registration desk just in time.

Dad and I missed the entire contest. By the time he had me cleaned up, it was over. The good news, though, was that my sister had won first place. Mom came running out of the auditorium, looking for Dad so she could tell him. While she was telling him and showing him the prizes my sister had won, one of the judges saw our family together and went back into the auditorium to speak with the other judges. A few minutes later the other two judges came to look at our family. You'll never guess what happened next. The judge who had seen Mom and Dad first had told the other judges that we were a black family. This was an important fact because one of the reasons my sister had won was that they thought she was a white baby. All of the other babies in the competition were white.

After a few minutes of discussion and asking my mom some rather embarrassing questions, the judges changed their ruling. They said that my sister was not eligible as a contestant because of her ethnic background, and therefore she was disqualified. The contest was for whites only. If Dad had been at the registration table, we would not have been allowed to register.

Dad comforted Mom as best he could because he knew that she

would get into trouble if he didn't. She wanted to give the contest organizers a piece of her mind, to say the least. But she didn't. Dad calmed her down, and we left. Dad knew what to do next. He took us to an ice cream shop and bought ice cream for everybody. This was the beginning of one of our family traditions: an ice cream, pop and potato chips celebration. Joyce and I still enjoy those today.

One day I scared the heck out of Daddy. On this particular occasion, we were living in a house at the corner of Watson and Rivard on the east side of Detroit. I was five years old, and Joyce was four. Dad had taken us across the street to the playground, and we were playing in the sandbox. Dad was sitting nearby on a bench, watching us play and reading the newspaper. I was playing with a ball, and it got away from me. It landed on the grass outside of the sandbox. I jumped out of the sandbox and ran to retrieve it. While I was on my way back to the sandbox with the ball, Dad picked me up and said, "Oh, my God. I must get you to a doctor. Come on, Joyce, follow me." He grabbed Joyce by the hand and was walking really fast. Dad could walk faster than most people could run. The two of us clung to him for dear life. We didn't know why he was so upset.

When we got to our house, he yelled for Mom, "Nettie Mae, get out here now. Roz has a bad cut on her foot." Mom came running out and saw the blood running from my foot and said, "Let's go." The doctor's office was on the corner of our street. When we got there, the nurse met us at the door. She ushered us into a room where we all sat and waited. While we were waiting, my dad explained to my mother what had happened. When I had jumped out of the sandbox, I had cut my foot on a piece of glass lying in the grass. I didn't know it, but Dad knew because he saw me leaving a trail of blood with every step I took. So he just snatched me up, grabbed Joyce and made a dash for it. When the doctor came into the examining room, he looked at my foot and said, "Oh my, this is quite a cut. She's going to need stitches." He turned to my dad and asked, "How did this happen?" Dad said, "She cut her foot on a piece of glass on the playground." The doctor said, "She'll need about eight or nine stitches, but she'll be fine." He stitched me up, and Daddy carried me home. I didn't even know what had happened until Dad explained it to the doctor. Through it all, I wasn't worried. When Dad picked me up and held me in his arms, I knew that everything was going to be all right. Dad was my comfort zone.

When I was little, I always wondered why Dad wore long-sleeved shirts no matter how hot or cold it was. One day I asked Mom. She said, "Well, according to his sister, Louella, your father did something he shouldn't have when he was a little boy and got scalded. It left scars on his arm. He wears long sleeves so no one will see the scars." I said, "Did she tell you how he got scalded?" She said, "Nope. Louella doesn't talk much about the things that happened in their family." I said, "Do you think Dad would tell me if I asked?" She said, "He might. Go and ask him." So I did. I found him in his bedroom and asked, "Dad, why do you always wear long-sleeved shirts? Mom said you were scalded when you were little. She said Louella said that. Is that true?" Dad looked at me with a silly grin and said, "If my sister said that, then it must be the truth."

I said, "So what happened?" He said, "Awww, Pretty Girl, I don't really remember what happened. It was so long ago. All I remember is that Louella was watching me, and she was trying to cook for us. Something spilled, and I was in the way, and that's all I remember. I do know, though, that when my mother came home, she took Louella into another room and gave her a heck of a spanking. I felt so sorry for her. My mom didn't have to do that. It was an accident. My brothers and I didn't get to say anything because my mother didn't want to hear it. After she finished spanking Louella, she made us all go to bed." I told Dad that must run in the family because Mom did the same thing. He laughed and said, "Don't tell your mom." I said, "Okay, Dad. I won't tell. I'm not telling Joyce either. If she wants to know, she'd better ask."

On another day Aunt Louella was at the house when my sister came running into the house in tears because one of the boys she was playing with, Jimmy, had slapped her during an argument. Louella asked her what was wrong, and she said, "Jimmy slapped me." Louella told her, "Don't let anyone do that and get away with it. If they hit you, hit them back." Louella didn't know that this had happened a few days earlier. After talking to Louella, my sister went outside, ran up to

---

Jimmy and slapped him as hard as she could. Jimmy started crying. He was crying so loudly that Louella ran outside to see what was going on. Jimmy told her, "Joyce slapped me, and I didn't do anything!" Louella grabbed my sister and ran into the house laughing. She said, "I didn't mean for you to run out and slap Jimmy like that. You should only do that when he's about to do something to you." Then she gave Joyce a big hug, kissed her, and sent her back outside. My sister found Jimmy, apologized to him and gave him a big hug. Jimmy learned a lesson, too. He never slapped my sister again.

III

Family Favorites

Music has and always will play a significant role in the lives of our family. My maternal grandmother was the one who started Joyce and me singing and playing the piano. Mother was the choir director at her church in Birmingham, Alabama. When we were only four and five years old, we went to live with Mother temporarily because Mom had had major surgery that required a long recuperation period. We weren't interested in taking music lessons, but we knew that she wouldn't take no for an answer. Neither would Mom. If we had resisted in any way, we would have suffered the consequences because both Mother and Mom believed in what the Bible says: "Spare the rod, and spoil the child." We thank God today for Mother's lessons because both of us are good musicians.

Most people don't know that Dad was a good singer and had a baritone quality similar to Marvin Gaye and Sam Cooke. He was a smooth crooner. Dad was too shy to sing in public but enjoyed singing at home, on his everyday walks and at the barber shop. His favorite types of music were gospel, jazz, popular tunes and Negro spirituals. Songs like "Ain't Misbehavin'" (Fats Waller), "Dark Was the Night" (Blind Willie Johnson), "West End Blues" (Louis Armstrong) and songs from the Big Band era.

Dad would walk around the house singing songs and humming. One of his favorites, which we heard him singing often, was "Gimme Dat Ole Time Religion." This was a favorite among black Christians in the churches and during slavery. It was quite popular in the South and has become a part of the gospel genre known as Southern gospel.

Refrain:
    Gimme me dat ole time religion
    Gimme me dat ole time religion
    Gimme me dat ole time religion
    It's good enough for me.

Verse:
    It was good for my mother
    It was good for my mother
    It was good for my mother
    And it's good enough for me

Verse:
    It was good for my father...
    It was good for my sister...

The refrain would remain the same throughout the song, but the verses would change depending on how the singer or performing group felt. This improvisation is a common tradition with gospel singing that has been passed down through the ages. Dad was in keeping with the tradition. When we became old enough to sing, we would sing it with him, much to Mom's enjoyment. She would clap and stomp her feet to the rhythm. Dad didn't realize it at the time, but he was our first gospel music teacher. Gospel music is one of my favorites, and I thank Dad for getting me started. I direct, sing and play gospel music in several choirs and churches, and it is always a part of my musical repertoire. Gospel music is here to stay.

The best times to hear Dad singing "Ole Time Religion" were on the porch during the warm months, on Sundays and while he was taking a bath. When he sang in the bathroom, Joyce and I would stand in the hallway and listen. We didn't want him to know we were listening because then he would stop singing. We enjoyed hearing him sing.

Another of Dad's favorites was "Pretty Girl," a popular tune in Dad's era. I can't remember which male group sang "Pretty Girl" back in the day, waaayyy back in the day. You could tell that it was one of Dad's favorites by the way he would sing it. He would put his heart and soul into it. That song gave me the nickname that Dad had for me, "Pretty Girl."

Mom couldn't sing at all, but she could play the piano. She would tell stories about how she and her girlfriend auditioned for the choir in high school. After the audition, she asked the choir instructor what voice she could sing, and the instructor replied, "Dog text." That hurt my mother's feelings, and she never sang another note while she was in school. She was so embarrassed. She made up for that later with us. When people ask us where we got our singing voices, we would say from our father. Not to be left out, my mother would say, "Yes, they got their singing voices from their father, but they got their brains from me." We tried many times to get Dad to sing in church, but he wouldn't. He was satisfied with just singing in the background. I wonder if he sang when he was a kid.

Mom continued the piano lessons for Joyce and me that Mother had started when we were living in Birmingham, Alabama. This worked out well for our family because Mom would accompany us on the piano while Dad, Joyce and I sang. Dad enjoyed this as much as we did at our home, but we just couldn't get him to sing with us at public gatherings. In retrospect I think we should have nudged him a little bit more and maybe, just maybe, he would have done it. Then we would have been known as the Stearnes Trio—Joyce a soprano, me an alto and Dad a baritone. That would have been awesome.

Joyce and I have been singing since elementary school in choirs, at churches and in other musical groups. Mom and Dad always supported us in our musical endeavors. They always came to our programs to hear us sing and play. When I was performing, I always looked for my dad in the audience. He was my comfort zone. He would always sit in the back because he didn't like crowds, but he'd let us know he was there.

Besides performing music together, our family enjoyed listening to music on the 33⅓s, 78s and the small 45s that were popular. Those were big, black, vinyl records played on record players, unlike the music of today. Those were the good old days, and the records were breakable, unlike the recordings of today. They were also cheap, and we had stacks of them. We bought records every week, just like kids download tunes today. Dad loved those records. When we would hear him singing, sometimes we would join in and sometimes just listen.

Fans Called Him "Turkey," I Called Him Dad

Our family loves to play games, outdoors or indoors; it didn't matter. Dad would join us when he could. He didn't play softball with us, though, because he thought we would get hurt. He said girls shouldn't play softball, but we did anyway. He was at every game, standing on the sidelines and giving us pointers.

Dad loved playing board games and card games. Pinochle, Bid Whist, Checkers, Chinese Checkers and Monopoly were his favorites. The game we played with Dad most often was pinochle. It was a lot of fun. I had to be Dad's pinochle partner because when he made a mistake, Mom would yell and fuss at him and hurt his feelings. When she did that, depending on his mood, he would switch partners or quit. One of the mistakes he would make every time, which drove all of us crazy, was not passing his aces to his partner. In this version of pinochle that we often played, players could pass four cards to their partner if their team got the bid. The idea is that you would pass four cards to your partner that would help your partner make the bid. Then your partner would counter by passing to you four cards that your partner didn't need. The best cards in this game are aces. Dad would have aces in his hand and wouldn't pass them to his partner. He said, "I know my aces are going to turn. I want to turn them myself." This would infuriate my mom. Joyce and I would laugh. Then I would say, "That's okay, Dad, play with me." Dad and I played as partners a lot just to keep the peace. Plus, I enjoyed playing with Dad. We lost a lot of games, but it was fun. You needed four people to play, and we had four in our family, so that worked out well. The more I think about it, I think Dad refused to pass his aces just to tease Mom. He was having fun, and so were we. The family that plays together, stays together. To this day, my sister and I still play pinochle every Wednesday as volunteers at the senior center in Auburn Hills, Michigan (but not the same version).

IV

It Takes a Village
to Raise a Child

"It takes a village to raise a child." When you hear these words, take them to heart. Tradition speaks for itself. Back in the day, communities were the hub of society. Everyone learned how to interact with each other in positive ways that enhanced learning and the development of skills. Our family was blessed to have experienced this in our neighborhoods on the east and west sides of Detroit. That sense of community was instrumental in making us the people that we are today.

When I say it takes a village to raise a child, that comes from personal experience. All of my life my parents instilled in us the importance of family and community. If memory serves me correctly, our first home was on the east side of Detroit in a house near the corner of Watson and Rivard. We lived across the street from the Eastern Market and a few blocks away from what was then known as Black Bottom, which was a neighborhood predominantly populated by black residents and businesses, including nightclubs well known for their blues, Big Band and jazz performers. Black Bottom was destroyed intentionally to make way in the 1960s for what is currently known as the Fisher Freeway. This was comparable to what happened to Black Wall Street in Tulsa, Oklahoma, without the violence and devastation. The communities and businesses were destroyed, never to return again. We lived in that neighborhood from 1948 to 1953.

It was a good neighborhood, and several of our family members lived in close proximity. One of my mother's younger sisters, Eleanor, and her family lived only two blocks away from us. My dad's sister, Louella, and brother Bennie lived on the same block as we did; so did a few of our cousins.

Our house was what I called the "family house." I say this because Dad and Mom opened our home to any family member who needed assistance for as long as was necessary. Our home was a revolving door for members of our family and for folks that we considered family. Back in the day, this was a common tradition. Families took care of each other, and we were better for it. Dad and Mom worked together to make sure that everyone felt like this was their home. Dad was the breadwinner and Mom the homemaker. Joyce and I are who we are today because of their influence. So are many of our family members and relatives who lived in the "family house."

While we were living on the east side, Dad played a key role in keeping our family together. Louella would babysit and help Mom with the chores while Bennie would help Dad. During these times Joyce and I were still toddlers, so the help my aunt and uncle offered was much appreciated by Mom and Dad. Those were the good old days. We ate breakfast, lunch and dinner together as a family at the same time every day. Dad would sit at the head of the table and Mom would sit to his right and whoever else was in the house at the time would join in. Dad wasn't there for breakfast and lunch because he was at work, but he was always there for dinner. He would lead us in prayer before we ate, then Mom would make everyone at the table, including Dad, say a Bible verse from memory. Each person had to come up with a different verse because Mom would spank anyone who repeated someone else's verse. This was a tradition started by my maternal grandmother.

In my teenage years, I always thought that because Dad had said the prayer, he shouldn't have had to say a Bible verse too. That was just a thought. I never said anything to Mom about this because there were some things that I knew I couldn't or shouldn't say, so I just kept it to myself.

Case in point: Mom told me a story about one of her brothers, Alphonso, who spoke at the dinner table and later regretted it. My mom, her parents and her 11 siblings were sitting at the dinner table. Each one took a turn saying a Bible verse. When Alphonso's turn came, he said, "Jesus wept, Moses crept, Peter fell down the back door-step." Laughter filled the room. In the blink of an eye, my grandmother literally threw a book at him and made him get up from the table and go to his room. She punished him by not allowing him to finish his supper. He never made that mistake again. Sitting at the dining room table with family and friends was a common occurrence and one that I miss doing today.

In September 1953, our family moved from the east side across from the Eastern Market to the west side at 2689 Carter. Joyce and I were five and six years old, respectively. That proved to be our family's last move. Dad didn't like moving, and the rest of us didn't either, but it was a good move. Currently, the Carter house is a historic site with a family unrelated to us living there.

Our transition to the new neighborhood was fairly easy. It was a diverse neighborhood, and the residents on our block were like a family for each other. The black business owners also treated the residents like family. Black-owned businesses were the heart of the community in our west-side neighborhood. They encompassed a 15-block area up and down Linwood from Joy Road to West Grand Boulevard.

One of my most lasting impressions of Dad was his ability not only to purchase the house but also to pay the mortgage in full in half the time allotted. That was an amazing accomplishment for a man who had made it through the many crises of his era. Here we had a man whose father died when he was young, whose mother had to raise him and his siblings on her own during a time when black people were treated less than human and who had to drop out of school and get a job to help his family survive. Dad never attended college and had no formal financial education but knew how to manage money. Today Dad would be able to purchase anything he wanted because, after a credit check, he would be approved automatically. He bought a house, bought cars and paid cash for the cars. We never went hungry or needed anything even when he was laid off for two weeks by Ford at Christmas. My dad accomplished more than many of the people I know and did it with humility. He was *amazing*.

As a young girl, I thought Dad was stingy. Whenever Joyce and I asked for money, we had to listen to a long, drawn-out story about how to spend money. Then he would give it to us. As I came of age, a light bulb went off in my head. Duh. Dad had the best credit of anyone I ever knew. He always paid his bills on time. Most of the time, he would pay them in full. Unlike Mom, he didn't like credit or credit cards. My mother liked having credit cards because she didn't want to pay cash. She would use a credit card for large purchases and then try to persuade Dad that it was the right thing to do.

They didn't argue much, but when they did, it was generally about money and Mom's use of credit cards. Dad paid cash for just about everything. His credit was so good that when new department stores opened, such as Hudson's or Kern's, they would send Dad a credit card in the mail. All he had to do was to sign the paperwork and send it back. If Dad saw them before Mom, he would take the cards, cut them up and put them into the garbage. When Mom would open a credit account, Dad would do all he could to pay it off in a short period of time. He never wanted to pay late fees or to be charged interest. He felt that was a waste of money.

After moving to the west side, Dad continued with his daily routine. During the cold months, he would stop after work at the corner store and bring us potato chips and pop, one each for my sister and me. During the warmer months, he would bring us ice cream, potato chips and pop. We would see him coming down the street and run and jump into his arms. He would carry us and the goodies down to the house. He did this until we were teenagers. After we became teenagers, we would just run and meet him, give him a kiss on the cheek and help carry the goodies ourselves. No other dad on the block did this. The other kids would make jokes, but we chose to ignore them. We knew that they were jealous and wished that their dads would do what our dad was doing.

Whenever Dad arrived home from work, he would greet Mom, take a bath, eat dinner and go for a walk. Then every night when Dad knew that everyone in the house was asleep, he would come to everyone's room with a flashlight and shine it in your face to see if you were okay. Then he would walk around the house and check all of the windows and doors to make sure that they were locked and that everyone was safe. We never asked him why he did this, but Mom said that she thought that something might have happened in his childhood that made him safety conscious or maybe because he was born at a time when black people were constantly in fear of something bizarre happening to them and their families because of racist practices during his lifetime.

During the early months of my pregnancy, while my husband and I were living with my parents, Dad shining the flashlight in our faces came in handy. Every night during my pregnancy, instead of cravings like most pregnant women have, I would get charley horses, and at times they were very painful. I didn't know what to do, so I would just lie there suffering and hoping the pains would go away. One night, Dad was making his usual rounds with his flashlight. When he came to my room, he heard me moaning and groaning and said, "Pretty Girl, what's wrong?" I said, "Dad, I've got a charley horse in both legs and they hurt." He said, "Get up. You have to work them out." I said, "I can't. I might fall. Dad, help me! They hurt."

Dad got closer and saw the tears in my eyes. He put the flashlight down on my bed and said in a loud voice, "Get up!!" I refused. Then Dad pulled me up and made me stand on my feet. He grabbed both of my hands and said, "Pretty Girl, you have got to walk. Stop crying. I know what I'm doing. You can't just lie in the bed and hope they will go away. Walk!" I could see that Dad wasn't going to take no for an answer, so I started walking.

Dad was right. After I started walking, the pain subsided and gradually went away. After all of the pain was gone, I said, "Dad, you mean to tell me that I have been lying here every night suffering, and all I had to do was get up and walk? Why didn't you tell me this sooner?" Dad chuckled and said, "I didn't know you were having charley horses. How long has this been going on?" I said, "Every night since I've been pregnant." He said, "Now you know what to do." We hugged and said good night. Dad watched while I got back into bed. Then he picked up his flashlight and continued with his rounds. I'm so glad

Dad asserted himself in making me accept his solution to my charley horse situation. What a relief that was.

In my younger days, Dad hated confrontations. I seldom saw him angry or upset. He stayed calm even when the rest of us were running around like chickens with our heads cut off. A few years after our move to the west side, we had a few neighborly squabbles but nothing serious. One of these involved Mr. Lillard and his son, Ralph. When Mom had to take care of some business and left my sister and me with Dad, he went into the kitchen to get something to drink while we were playing. There was a knock at the door, and Joyce and I ran to answer it. It was one of our neighbors, Mr. Lillard. He came in and asked if our parents were at home. I said, "Mom is not here, but Dad is in the kitchen." I called Dad and said that Mr. Lillard wanted to talk to him. Dad told us to have him come back later. Whenever Dad sensed that someone wanted to talk about something confrontational, he always let my mom handle it. She would decide if he needed to be involved or not. Most of the time she would handle it.

We told Mr. Lillard what Dad had said. He pushed past us, walked over to Dad and said, "It's about your daughters. We need to talk." Dad said, "Girls, go up to your room. I need to talk to Mr. Lillard." I looked at Joyce and said, "Uh-oh. I think we're in trouble. Wish Mom were here." While Dad talked with Mr. Lillard, we were standing near the top of the stairs so we could hear what they were saying. We thought Dad wouldn't know we were there. If he had, we really would have been in trouble for not obeying him. We heard Mr. Lillard say, "Your daughters double teamed my son, Ralph, and beat him up because he won the Monopoly game they were playing. Your daughters were upset and said that he had cheated. They said he wouldn't have won if he hadn't cheated because he doesn't know how to count. Then they jumped on him." My dad said, "My girls are not vicious like that. If they jumped on your son, they had a particularly good reason or he must have started it." Mr. Lillard said, "I'll prove it. I'll be right back." He left, got his son and returned.

Meanwhile, my dad told us to hurry downstairs and said, "I know you've been listening. so bring your butts down here now. You're not slick." He was so mad. Now we knew we were in trouble. By this time, the neighbor was back and came through the door with his son. Dad had left the door unlocked. When he came back with Ralph, the boy said, "Mr. Stearnes, your daughters did jump on me. Look at my face. My dad told me what they said, and they lied. They're mean. I'm not playing with them anymore." Dad was furious. He said, "Girls, did you jump on this boy and beat him up like he said?"

We said, "No, Dad. He's lying. And besides, look at him! He's older than us and bigger too. Wait until Mom gets here because she knows what happened. They already talked to Mom about it, and she thought it was settled. Ralph hit Joyce first because he was mad that she had bought houses on Park Place and Boardwalk, and he landed on Park Place and went bankrupt. He said we cheated, jumped up and slapped Joyce. Then I punched him, and he fell. He rolled over, and when he got up, he ran out of the house crying and saying that he was going to tell his dad and that we were going to be in trouble. Ralph and his dad already talked with Mom, and she knew Ralph was lying and let it go. Wait until she comes home. She'll tell you." Dad told them to leave and that he would take care of it and wouldn't let it happen again. The neighbor said, "Thank you, Mr. Stearnes. They need a spanking." My dad said, "Yep, they probably do. Thanks for telling me what happened."

After they left, Dad closed the door and took off his belt. We started crying and begging him not to whoop us because we hadn't done anything wrong. We kept saying, "Dad, we didn't do it. Wait until Mom gets here, and you'll see." Dad said, "That was so embarrassing. The two of you know better. You know I don't like fighting. Go upstairs to your room." We ran up the stairs with tears in our eyes, and Dad came behind us to our room and spanked us. We really cried. Dad hurt our feelings because he didn't believe us. We cried more about that than about the spanking.

When Mom got home, we were in our room still crying and sniffling. She asked us what happened. Dad was in his room down the hall watching TV. When he heard Mom talking to us, he came to our room. She said, "Turk, what happened? Why are the girls crying? Did you spank them?" He said, "Yes," and he told her how Mr. Lillard and his son were so convincing that he had to spank us as a punishment for fighting, especially since Ralph was one of our friends. Mom stood there with her hands on her hips and said, "Turk, your daughters were telling you the truth. If you had asked some of the other children who were playing with them, you would have known that Ralph was lying. He's a troublemaker. Didn't they tell you the whole story?" Dad said, "No, they just kept saying, 'Wait until Mom gets home. She'll tell you.'"

Dad came over to us, put his arms around us and said, "Oh, my goodness, sweeties. I'm so sorry." He hugged and rocked us for a while, and that made us feel a lot better. Hugging was something Mom and Dad always did, and it really made us feel comfortable, secure and loved. Hugging was a great thing in our family. After we calmed down and stopped crying, Dad said, "From now on, Nettie Mae, you do the spanking. These are my girls. I don't want to hurt them like this again." Then he left. We said, "Mom, where is Dad going?" She said, "I don't know. Did you eat?" We said, "Nope." She said, "Come on. Let's go downstairs and get something to eat. Then you can watch a little TV and get ready for bed."

While we were watching TV, Dad came back into the house; and guess what? He had gone to the corner store and bought our favorite snacks: ice cream, potato chips and pop. He brought some for us and some for Mom. He apologized again, gave us a hug and said, "Good night, Bugsy and Pretty Girl. I'm going to bed. I have to go to work in the morning." We could tell that Dad was sorry for what he had done because he had such a sad look on his face. We knew he wasn't going to spank us again. One thing we could count on was that Dad was a man of his word. After that incident, he never spanked us again. Mom did all the spanking.

Dad did discourage us from two activities though: climbing trees and sitting on top of our garage. In our next-door neighbor's backyard were a mulberry tree about 10 feet tall and a skinny tree that was about seven feet tall. Both of these had branches overhanging into our backyard. Some of the branches of the skinny tree reached to our garage. Joyce and I and some of our friends would climb as high as we could in the mulberry tree to gather mulberries to eat and to give Mom so that she could make mulberry pies. Those pies were sooo good! And so were the mulberries. We also liked to climb the skinny tree so we could sit on top of the garage and play games there. Something about sitting on top of the garage made us feel like we were sitting on top of the world.

Sometimes, when Dad was coming home from work, he would come walking down the street. When he did that, we would run to meet him and to help bring the goodies he was carrying to the house. Then, at other times, he would walk down the alley and come through the backyard. Then we would be either in the mulberry tree or sitting on top of the garage with our playmates. Dad would always be surprised when he spotted us there. We thought this was funny, but Dad didn't. He would have a disgruntled look on his face when he would hear us call out, "Hi, Dad. We're up here!" He would look in the direction of our voices and say, "Girls aren't supposed to climb trees or be on top of garages. That's dangerous. What the heck are you doing up there? Get down here *now*!!!" We would hurry down and run over to Dad and give him a hug, hoping this was enough to keep us out of trouble. That worked. Dad loved getting hugs and kisses from his girls.

Dad liked to take a walk every day after work. His favorite stop along the way was at the local barber shop. On the east side, where we first lived, he would stop at the barber shop on Hastings. On the west side, he would stop at the one on Linwood. He loved talking about baseball and his family. So did the guys in the shop. My dad wasn't much of a talker, but if you wanted him to say something, all you had to do was talk about baseball, and he would be off and running.

Kids today don't have the interest in baseball that we had. They are more fascinated with football and basketball. Most of the baseball fields have been demolished or turned into basketball courts and football fields. In the 1950s and 1960s, baseball was one of the most popular sports in Detroit. There were baseball diamonds all over the city on playgrounds and on the fields behind every school.

In our neighborhood, baseball was the favorite thing to do, especially when school was out for the summer. We played on the sidewalks, in the street, in the alley and on the baseball diamonds as often as we could. We formed two teams on our block on Carter and played against the other teams in our neighborhood. Because there weren't enough girls to have their own separate team, each team was composed of both boys and girls. My sister, Mom and I were always on the same team. Mom was a good ballplayer, too, and a heck of a pitcher. Sometimes she would pitch for our team. Because she looked so young, a lot of the guys thought she was our sister. To fool the other team, especially the kids who didn't know us, she would dress like us. We couldn't afford uniforms, so we would wear blouses and shorts or jeans of the same color.

When Mom was pitching, Dad would cheer from the sidelines and go along with the deception. He thought it was funny. He couldn't figure out why the other team didn't know that a grown woman, our mom, was on the pitcher's mound. The deception would work until one of the players on the other team would say something obnoxious or call Mom a name, and then our team would be ready for a fight. Dad would step in and stop the ruckus. Joyce and I would let them know who they were talking to and that they couldn't talk to our mom like that. You should have seen the looks on their faces. As expected, they would apologize and everyone would have a good laugh. After an incident like this, word would get around and the other teams wouldn't be so easily deceived. But it was fun while it lasted.

Because the boys outnumbered the girls four to one in our neighborhood, we had no choice but to do what they did. The girls played just as hard as the boys, thus the tag "tomboys." We didn't mind the tag. We took it as a positive and enjoyed being called tomboys, my sister and I especially. We tried to make up for the fact that Dad had no sons. It came in handy that we had all of the baseball equipment. We used that as leverage to make the boys play some of the games that the girls wanted to play, which included Hopscotch, Jacks, and Red Light Green Light. Last but not least, we made them play house. The boys hated it, but the girls loved it.

Throughout elementary school and into high school, Joyce and I were tomboys. We have passed some of those attributes on to some of the younger girls in our family. Dad encouraged this, especially because baseball was our first love. We played baseball as often as the weather would allow, and we were good at it. Joyce played shortstop. I switched between first baseman, pitcher and hind catcher, which is another name for catcher. I tried centerfield because my dad had played centerfield, but playing with females taught me that most of the action was in the infield. Most females have difficulty hitting to the outfield, and when they do, it's usually a very catchable fly ball.

My greatest moment was when my dad saw me hit a home run. He told me later, "Pretty Girl, you hit just like me." At the next game, my coaches told my dad that they wished he had never said that because they couldn't do a thing with me. I was one of the best hitters on the team, but hearing Dad say that just made my day. I needed and wanted his approval. I wanted him to know that Joyce and I loved the game almost as much as he did and that we would do everything we could to make him proud.

We played on several teams, and Dad came to all our games whenever possible. We always looked forward to seeing Dad, and he would come even if he had to walk to the playing field. We didn't have a car, and Dad didn't like depending on other people. So, if the bus wasn't on time, he walked. Dad was always on time. You could set your clock by him. He was not a "CP time" (colored people's time) person, and I loved that about him.

One day, we were playing ball in the alley near the corner from where we lived next to an apartment building. It was my turn at bat. I hit the ball and started running towards first base. As I was running, I saw Dad coming down the alley about a quarter block away with Nicky, our dog. Nicky saw one of the guys, Gregory, trying to tag me with the ball. Nicky ran and grabbed him by his pant leg. He held him, growling, until I crossed home plate. Dad just stood and watched with a smile on his face. After I crossed home plate, I said, "Nicky, let Gregory go. I'm okay." Gregory said, "Mr. Stearnes, you know that's not fair. That's cheating. A dog can't play ball." Dad laughed and put Nicky back on his leash, and they went home. That was the end of the game. We won, and the other team cried, "Cheaters! Next time we'll play on the field so your dog can't hold anybody." Dad thought it was hilarious, and so did my team. He rewarded Nicky with a ham bone and a piece of chicken.

At another game, I hit what should have been a home run, and I was casually running around the bases because I had hit the ball over the centerfielder's head. What I didn't realize was that she was fast and had picked up the ball and was running back with it in hand, hoping to throw me out. When I looked up and saw her coming, I was almost at third base. I said to myself, "Oh, no, she's not going to rob me of my home run. This will win the game for us." So I started running faster. As I rounded third, I looked up and saw this 200-pound female hind catcher trying to block the plate. What she didn't expect is what I did next. I was determined to make it home safely. So I picked up speed, slid in between her legs, and crossed the plate on the ground. I surprised the heck out of her. When she caught the ball, she was expecting me to run into her standing up. But I slid right between her legs. Then, to my surprise, she reached down with the ball in her glove and hit me hard on the nose. My right leg crossed the plate before the tag and the umpire yelled, "Safe!"

My teammates were running and jumping up and down. I didn't notice that my face and T-shirt were bloody. When one of my teammates helped me up, blood squirted everywhere. Somebody screamed. I looked down to see where the blood was coming from, not realizing that holding my head down made it worse. Then they noticed that there was blood all over my face. The front of my white T-shirt was covered with blood. While they were pulling me up to congratulate me and to have me join in the celebration, they could see the blood. Then we all realized that the hind catcher had tagged me so hard that it looked as though she had broken my nose.

My teammates picked me up while Dad came over and checked to see if I was okay. After taking a closer look, he saw that my nose was just badly bruised, not broken. I was too excited to worry about what had happened. My home run had won the game. Hallelujah! After all, what was a little blood? Dad put his arms around me, comforted me and said, "Pretty Girl, girls don't slide." I said, "Dad, you told me to do what it takes to win, and that's what I did." He laughed, put his handkerchief on my nose to help stop the bleeding and helped to brush the dirt off. Once the bleeding stopped, we gathered up my equipment, said our goodbyes and happily walked home. That was a very good day.

I liked the hind catcher position because I usually could persuade the umpires to make calls the way I wanted them to. For example, when the ball would come across the plate, I would say something like, "Oh, that was a good one." Then the umpire would say, "Strike." Or I would say, "Oops, you missed the plate" or "Not so good." Then the umpire would say, "Ball." At one game we were playing (and we were playing one of the best teams in the league), I was the hind catcher and the batter at the plate heard me say something. The umpire agreed with what I said, so the batter got upset, stepped away from the plate and said, "Who is the umpire, you or her?" Of course, that didn't sit well with the umpire, so when the next pitch crossed the plate, the umpire called, "Strike" and the batter struck out. That was the batter's first strikeout, and boy, was she pissed! But what could she do? After what had just happened, she couldn't afford to antagonize the ump again, so she swallowed her pride, mumbled something under her breath and angrily walked back to the dugout. In our day, you didn't mess with the umpires or boldly show your temper. The umpires had control, and if you wanted to win, you chalked it up to experience. I always said and would tell my teammates, "When the umpire makes a bad call, don't get mad, get even."

Both Dad and I have had occasion to apply that motto when we've had to deal with racially discriminatory situations. While I was attending Hutchins Junior High School in Detroit, I discovered that I was an exceptional speller. I was a contestant in the spelling bees at the school for three years, starting in the seventh grade. That first year I won my class spelling bee, the spelling bee for the school and then went to the regional bee to represent my school district. At the regional bee, I overheard a white lady tell her daughter, "I know you're not going to let these niggers beat you, are you?" I found my mom and told her what I had heard. I said, "Mom, if I don't beat anybody else in this competition, I'm going to beat her." After a couple of hours of competition, the contest came down to the white girl and me. I won. My winning streak continued for the next two years. At each regional bee, she and I were always the last two standing. I won every time. Even at that age, I was already a competitive person and always wanted to do my best. Comments like that would "ig" me on. I'm pretty sure that Dad had many similar encounters and rose above them in the same way.

Hutchins Junior High School was only six blocks away from our home on Carter, so we walked to school every day. When I graduated from Hutchins and went to Cass Technical High School, I had to ride the bus because Cass was not in walking distance.

After I graduated from Cass Tech, the house on Carter became the new "family house." Several of our relatives can attest to that. One of those was my mom's sister Ruth. Aunt Ruth was having some problems, so she called Mom to see if she could come and stay with us. Mom ran the request by Dad. As usual, he said, "No problem. We'll make room." Several weeks later Ruth came with her three daughters, Syrennia, Jamelle and Deidre. This started another family adventure in the "family house."

Ruth was a singer, so she fit right in with our musical family. She hadn't known that Dad could sing and was pleasantly surprised when she found out that he could. One day she overheard him singing "Ole Time Religion" in his bedroom and was amazed at how good he sounded. From then on, she tried to encourage him to sing at church, but to no avail. He was happy just singing at home and during his daily walks.

Mom and I knew that the three sisters, Syrennia, age six, Jamelle, age five, and Deidre, age three, were old enough for us to determine whether they had any musical ability, especially singing. So we started teaching them songs to sing, and they learned with Dad's encouragement. The three of them would sit on Dad's lap in the dining room, where the piano was, and would sing there or go up to his room to sing. They felt more comfortable when Dad was around because Mom was the disciplinarian. If the learning wasn't happening the way that Mom felt it should, she would give them "the look," and that would straighten them up. We all knew what that look meant. Dad wouldn't say a word. He would wait to see what happened next. There were only a few times when he had to intervene; when he did, he caught the blues from Mom.

Dad really enjoyed having these little girls in our home. He spent as much time with them as he would with his grandchildren. When it came to the children in our family, whether immediate family members or not, their parents could always count on Dad for support. Whenever I would get the three girls together for a music lesson at home to practice for singing at church or another program, Deidre, who was the youngest, needed a little more attention than her older sisters. They were quicker learners than Deidre. To compensate, Dad would sit Deidre on his lap and sing the songs to her. He would do this as often as his schedule would allow so that by the time her sisters were ready to perform, Deidre would be ready, too. Dad refused to let Deidre miss out on performing with her sisters. They were like the Three Stooges, only better.

Aunt Ruth and her daughters lived with us for a year, then moved into their own home on Stoepel on the northwest side of Detroit. The bond that we developed has served as an example for others to follow. Syrennia, Jamelle and Deidre treasure the relationship that they had with Dad and to this day have many fond memories of him.

Syrennia, whom we called Rennie (pronounced Reenie), recently shared some of her memories with me. She said that she and her sisters called Dad "Uncle Turk" and Mom "Aunt Nettie." I knew that. I just wanted to see if she remembered. In her own words, she said, "Uncle Turk was quiet and was the sweetest and most gentle giant that we had ever met. He towered over us, but he was always warm and friendly and would laugh at our antics.

"Uncle Turk worked at the neighborhood laundromat, where he made sure that everything was clean and that the machines were in good working order. Even though he was volunteering to work, he seemed to take pride in ensuring that everything was well managed. I often asked Uncle Turk if I could accompany him to work; he always chuckled and said, 'Yes.' When we got there, I would ask for ice cream.

He would gladly buy me an ice cream bar from an ice cream freezer that rotated after a dime was inserted. I don't know why Jamelle and Deidre didn't go, but I was happy they didn't.

"I noticed something else about Uncle Turk. He loved his privacy. I recall that when he was not at home, his bedroom door was always locked. I was intrigued about what was inside, so, when he would come home, my sisters and I would knock on Uncle Turk's door and he would chuckle and peek out of his door to see who was knocking. Then he would open the door and let us in. We were so excited peering into his sacred space.

"I also noticed that he didn't eat a lot. Two of his favorite foods were any type of greens and corn bread. He'd take a whole white onion and bite into it like an apple. Then he would eat the greens behind that humongous bite. We loved Uncle Turk."

I remember the locked door as well. The reason for it was that Dad was responsible for keeping all of our family's important documents in a safe place. Dad and Mom didn't have a file cabinet, and there was no better place to put things. Dad kept those documents in an old trunk in his bedroom with a key lock on the door. His was the only room in the house that had a lock on the door. However, the funny thing is, Mom figured out how to unlock the key lock on the door. She figured that, as his wife, if she needed to get something from his room, she shouldn't have to wait until he got home. Without him knowing or maybe with his knowledge, she would get a flathead screwdriver and unscrew the screws that held the lock on the door. Then she would open the door, get what she needed, including money, and screw the lock back on the door. After she finished taking care of the business that prompted this action in the first place, she would return the documents, not the money, as though nothing had happened. Dad must have known that Mom was doing this, but I never heard him complain. He took it in stride.

V

Taking Things in Stride

Have you ever known or met someone who never complained about the difficult things that he was experiencing in his life? My dad was one of these people. Dad's job at the Ford River Rouge plant was in the worst department in the plant: the foundry. Anyone who could work there daily had to be a man of steel—physically and mentally. Employees there worked under horrendous conditions. The heat was tremendous, and the noise was extremely loud. That's why, when Dad retired, he had some hearing loss. I don't understand why, to this day, my mom and my dad didn't file a lawsuit against Ford for the deplorable working conditions that my dad and all the men working in the foundry were subjected to. Had I known then what I know now, I would have led the charge.

Despite the horrible working conditions, Dad never complained. You could set your clock by Dad. He went to work on time every day, Monday through Friday, and returned home every day at the same time. He was always clean and neat and never made excuses to get off work and never missed a day on his own.

Once he missed a day because of an accident on the line. One of the lines broke, and a piece of metal lodged in his leg. He had to be taken to the hospital. He stayed in the hospital for about a week and worried the nurses relentlessly about going home. He wanted to go back to work and his family. The day he was released, my mom went to get him. Because we didn't have a car, they took the bus. Dad was very frugal, so taking a cab was out of the question.

I wouldn't let a dog work in the foundry. When Dad went to work sick one day, I experienced the foundry firsthand. Dad was a very con-scientious man when it came to work, and he refused to call in sick. That's another lesson men today can learn. You would think under those circumstances, he gladly would have taken as much time off as he could get, but he didn't. Why? Because he was a man of integrity, and his word was his bond. If he said he was going to do something, he did it and did it to the best of his ability.

Early one morning Dad woke up and wasn't feeling well. He wasn't his usual ready-for-work self. Mom took his temperature and called for me. I was in my bedroom getting dressed for work. She said, "Your dad is sick. I'm going downstairs to make breakfast. Get the castor oil, give it to him, and make sure he stays in the bed until I come back up here." I got the castor oil out of the medicine cabinet in the bath-room. When I got back to his room, Dad was gone. While I was in the bathroom, Dad had dressed and had managed to slip down the stairs without us hearing him. I thought he was downstairs with Mom, so I asked her, "Mom, is Dad with you?" She said, "No, I thought he was in the bed. Didn't you give him the castor oil?" I said, "No, when I got it and came back to his room, he was gone." We ran outside hoping that we would catch him walking down the street, but he was gone. I ran back upstairs, finished dressing, ran out the door and got into my car. I drove to the bus stop, hoping that Dad was still there, but he wasn't. At that moment I knew Dad had caught the Linwood bus and was on his way to work.

I drove to the plant. When I got there, I had to figure out where the foundry was. When I went inside the foundry, the heat almost bowled me over. The noise was so loud that I couldn't hear myself think. I couldn't ask anybody where Dad was because no one could hear me. I had to just find him myself. I ran around that place because I was determined to find Dad and get the heck out of there before I caught on fire and went deaf in the process.

Luckily, Dad wasn't too far away. I found him leaning against a wall with a broom in his hand. He looked weak; sweat was running down his face, and his clothes were wet. I ran over to him and said, "Dad, we're leaving. You're too sick to work. Lean on me. I'll help you get out of here." He said, "Okay, Pretty Girl." One of the other guys saw us and came over to help. I was so glad. Dad was a little heavier than I thought. I didn't know how I was going to do it, but I was determined to get Dad out of that hellhole, especially because he was already sick and shouldn't have been there in the first place. This is another indication of the kind of man he was. How many people, now or then, would go to work sick? After I got Dad into the car, I said, "As long as I live, don't you ever try anything like that again! Your health is more important than this cotton-picking job."

To show how conscientious Dad was about being on time, especially for his job, I can recall an incident where Dad and one of our neighbors, Mr. Smith (that was actually his name), discovered that he and Dad both worked at the same Ford plant in River Rouge and had the same work schedule. After the discovery, Mr. Smith came to the house and told Dad that, since Dad didn't have a car, Mr. Smith wouldn't mind sharing his ride with Dad. He said they could ride together and he would love the company. They could ride home together as well. Dad thought about it and said, "OK. Since we have to be at work at 6:00 a.m., I'll be at your house at 5:00 a.m. You won't have to pick me up. I'll walk to your house." Mr. Smith said, "That'll be fine."

The next day, Dad walked to Mr. Smith's house and they rode to work together and came home together. I thought this was a good arrangement and was happy to see that now Dad wouldn't have to leave at 4:00 a.m. to take the bus to work to be there at 6. This arrangement worked out for several weeks but came to an abrupt halt. One day Dad arrived at Mr. Smith's home at the agreed upon time, and Mr. Smith wasn't quite ready. He had awakened a little bit later than usual and was running a little bit behind. Instead of being ready to leave at 5:00 a.m., he was ready at 5:30. Dad had no choice but to wait because if he had taken the bus, he wouldn't have gotten to work on time. Mr. Smith apologized, and they went to work.

The next day, Dad took the bus to work. When he came home, I asked him what happened to make him take the bus instead of riding with Mr. Smith. I indicated that I thought they had a good arrangement. He explained what had happened the day before and said that he had told Mr. Smith that he would not be riding with him to work anymore because he didn't want to be late. Dad thought leaving at 5:30 was not enough time to allow for incidental occurrences, which is why he left as early as he did. Dad said, as far as getting to work on time, he felt more comfortable riding on the bus. When I talked to Mr. Smith, he said he understood how Dad felt and they could still ride home together, which is what they did. That arrangement worked until Dad retired.

We became a Ford family and were proud of it while my father was still working at Ford. When my sister and I became old enough to drive and to purchase cars, we bought Ford cars. That was our way of showing support for Dad and union jobs. Some people would dispute that Ford cars are good. As a matter of fact, some people say that the word "Ford" stands for "Fix or Repair Daily." I know mechanics who say the same thing, but I tend to disagree. I love Ford cars and have had some real successes with them. I had a Ford Econoline van that I put over 450,000 miles on and never had any major problems with it. I loved that van. Dad loved it, too.

Dad's work at Ford Motor Company came with some fringe benefits for employees and their families during the holidays and when elementary schools let out for the summer. Ford would sponsor parties and picnics for the kids, and everything was free. The parties would be held at the Ford Rotunda in Dearborn, and the picnics were at Edgewater Amusement Park in Detroit. We were always excited to go to these events because they were a lot of fun. In my opinion, these were the best children's events given by any corporation. Ford really went all out for the kids. Whoever did the planning must have had a real love for children.

We didn't have a car, so Dad would take us to all of these events on the bus. Mom stayed home. I never asked her why she didn't join us, but I think it was because Dad really enjoyed taking us and liked riding the bus, especially with his girls. Rain, shine, sleet or snow, we didn't miss any of these events. Ford's age requirements were children ages five through 12 and accompanied by an adult.

For Ford's Halloween party, Joyce and I would dress up in

costumes that Mom made, but Dad would wear his regular clothes. He didn't want any part of dressing in a costume but loved seeing what my mother would come up with for us. At the party, there were all kinds of games and decorations, all the food you could eat, and candy, gifts, contests and a haunted house. The party lasted from 10:00 a.m. until 4:00 p.m. Dad, Joyce and I stayed the entire time, filling our bags with as much as the three of us could carry. I remember that these bags were given to us when we first came through the door and were made of a material comparable to the leather bags of today. They held a lot of stuff. After the party was over, we would get on the bus and go home. Joyce and I would be so tired that we would fall asleep on the ride home. Dad would have to carry us and the bags to our house once we got off the bus.

Ford's Christmas parties were even better than its Halloween parties. As we walked through the door, we felt as though we were in a winter wonderland. It was so magical. The highlight of the party was being able to sit on Santa's lap and telling him what we wanted for Christmas. There was an abundance of games, candy, food, toys and prizes, everything that a child could imagine wanting at a Christmas party. While we were checking out the sights, Dad would hold our hands and try to steer us to areas of the Rotunda that he thought we would enjoy most. We usually would follow Dad's lead, but a few times we would let go of his hand and take off. We would never go too far because we didn't want to make Dad mad. He was quiet but firm. He would allow us to run around just a little and to play with the other children, but he always stood in a position where he could keep an eye on us. Knowing Dad was there just added to our fun. After we had worn ourselves out, Dad would say, "Roz, Joyce, time to go." On the way out, we filled our bags with as much as we could carry. Dad would be loaded down. We would make our way to the bus, get in and go home. As usual, we would fall asleep on the bus. I don't know how Dad did it, but he managed to carry us and our overflowing bags to our house.

I thought we were in heaven at the Halloween and Christmas parties with Dad, but the best was yet to come. The Ford family picnics

---

at Edgewater Amusement Park were off the chain. Each picnic was an all-day affair, and everything was free. We caught the bus around 8:00 a.m. and didn't leave the park until 7:00 or 8:00 p.m. We would be exhausted.

Once we arrived at the park, it was a free-for-all. We could feel the excitement in the air and smell the aroma of the food. The grills were loaded with hot dogs, hamburgers, Polish sausages, knackwurst, corn on the cob, baked beans and barbecue ribs. Dad's favorites were the ribs and corn on the cob. We arrived and were ready to pig out. There was plenty of everything, and the rides were amazing. Dad was right there with us every step of the way. The lines were long, but we didn't mind. Dad would help get us in line, then find a seat and watch while we rode. Dad rode some of the rides with us but not the roller coaster. Despite our urging, he absolutely refused to get on it. After we had our fill of riding and eating or after Dad thought we had enough, he would gather us up with our things, hold our hands and escort us out of the park to the bus.

I remember one occasion when Dad saw the bus coming and we were about half a block away. It looked as though we were going to miss the bus. Dad started running and said, "Come on. We have to hurry. We don't want to miss the bus. There won't be another one for a while." Even though he was loaded down, Dad ran. So did we. We had trouble keeping up. Dad got to the bus stop in time to let the driver know that we weren't far behind. I knew in that moment why they called Dad "Turkey." He was fast! Dad could walk faster than most people could run. When Joyce and I got to the bus, our tongues were hanging out of our mouths and we were so exhausted that we could barely get up the steps. Dad had run with our packages and hadn't broken a sweat. He laughed and helped us to our seats. We slept all the way home, exhausted. Again, I don't know how he made it, but he did.

VI

Old School
Is the Best School

In our African American heritage, we have a saying, "Old school is the best school." What we mean by that is every generation should stick to the traditional values and moral obligations of its predecessors. I agree, and I'm sure my entire family would agree that we need to get back to doing things the old school way. It worked fine for us. Mom and Dad were old school.

When I say that Dad and Mom were old school, that about sums up our family's Christian beliefs. Our Christian beliefs and philosophies have been shared and demonstrated by our family in everything that we do. They continue to have significant impact in our everyday lives. We truly believe that the talents we have are God-given and that our successes are due to our faith. Dad was destined to become the legend he is today because of his faith. Faith is what keeps our family close. "The family that prays together, stays together."

Ever since I can remember, my family could always be found in church on Sunday mornings. Dad and Mom would escort us to church. If Joyce and I didn't go to church, we were not allowed to do anything else. Dad was a devout Baptist, and Mom was Lutheran. According to Mom, she and Dad agreed to compromise before we were born. They would take turns gong to each other's church. Quite often, though, Dad would give in and go to Mom's church. He wanted to keep the peace. After Joyce and I were born, transportation was an issue, so they agreed to go to whichever church was closest to home.

While we were living on Detroit's east side, Dad worked a lot of overtime and Sunday was his only day off. Many times, Dad wouldn't go to church because he was too tired and needed rest. Occasionally, Mom would go alone while Dad would babysit. Even when we were living temporarily with Mother, while Mom was recovering from major surgery, we went with Mother not only to church service every Sunday but also during the week to choir rehearsals. Mother, a Lutheran, was the choir director and in charge of all the music at her church. During this period, Dad would go to the Baptist church around the corner from the house in Detroit, but not often, because he had to care for Mom during her recovery.

After Mom recovered, Joyce and I came back to the east side and our family started attending Sacred Heart Catholic Church on Mack, which is still standing today. Mom and Dad chose Sacred Heart because it had an elementary school. They had been looking for another school for Joyce and me because Russell Elementary, the school we had been attending, had a lot of problems. There were a lot of fights at Russell. I remember one after which I came home with a torn dress and the ribbons missing from my hair. My opponent went home with a black eye. This was when Mom and Dad decided enough was enough. Meanwhile, the Baptist church around the corner was moving to a neighborhood with less violence, so Mom and Dad sent us to Sacred Heart for church and school. We were a Catholic family for two years.

Mom and Dad never got used to being Catholic, though. They didn't want to be baptized Catholic because they already had been baptized in their chosen religion. That was one of the reasons why we moved to the west side. On the west side, there were no Lutheran churches within walking distance, so, after scouring the neighborhood, Dad found a Baptist church on Blaine, a block from home. He told Mom, and they decided our family would go there. Going to a Baptist church was right up Dad's alley, and he got no argument from Mom. She just wanted us in church. Our family became members of New Mount Moriah Baptist Church and went every Sunday. Between Sunday School, church service and other activities of the congregation, the females in our family often spent most of the day in church, especially on the first Sunday of the month. Dad would attend the 11:00 a.m. service and any programs in which Joyce and I were participants. He didn't stay for the night activities because he had to get ready for work the next day. Dad would make sure that he got at least eight hours of sleep before leaving for work at 4:00 a.m. the next day. That was part of his daily routine.

I remember one time, when Joyce and I were in a program at church, the minister saw an opportunity to take up a collection because of the large crowd. He did so just as my dad was walking in the door. When he saw Dad, he said, "Ah, Mr. Stearnes is here. Mr. Stearnes, why don't you come up to the front and give us $20 as a thank you to the performers and the church staff? We would really appreciate your donation." The look on my dad's face was priceless. He was stunned and embarrassed. I didn't know what he was going to do because no one had ever done that to my dad before. After a slight pause, Dad walked to the front of the church, put a $20 bill into the basket and left the church. We were upset at my pastor for what he had just done to my dad. I wanted to punch him in the face. I knew, though, if I did, my mother would give me a spanking, so I managed to hold my peace.

When we got home, Dad said, "Pretty Girl and Bugsy, I love you and always want to be there for you, but I am never stepping foot in that sanctuary again as long as that pastor is there. When you are on a program, I will stay in the vestibule until you finish and then leave. He's not one of the good guys." We ran over to Dad and gave him a hug and said, "Don't worry, Dad. Mom will get him." And she did. The next time she saw the pastor, she gave him a good piece of her mind. She told him that he had no business asking Dad for a donation and then telling him what to give in front of the congregation. She said, "What if he hadn't $20 or no money at all? That was embarrassing! It would have been better if you had just pulled him over to the side and just asked for a donation. He would have been happy to do that, but you put my husband on front street. You'll never get a chance to do that again. My daughters are just as upset as I am." Of course, the pastor didn't see anything wrong with what he had done and tried to make excuses.

Mom didn't let him off the hook. After this incident, Dad would come to the church only for major events. He became what we call a CME Christian: Christmas, Mother's Day and Easter.

Several years later, when my sister and I were adults, this same pastor sent a note to my mother to tell her to meet him in his office. When she got there, he closed the door. I was walking past his office and saw that the door was partially opened. I went to close it, but while I was doing that, I overheard him say, "Mrs. Stearnes, you know you are a good-looking woman. I have had my eye on you for some time. Think maybe we could do a little something?" My mother was livid. She said, "First of all, I am a married woman and take my vows seriously. Second, you are a married man and shouldn't even be talking to me like that. Third, what would your wife say?" He was taken aback a bit but continued by saying, "Oh, speaking of marriage, I hear your daughter, Rosilyn, is getting married. I want to know if she is going to have the wedding here."

At that point I opened the door with a bang and said, "After what I just heard, not only am I not getting married here, especially with you as the minister, but I am going home and telling my dad that you were trying to hit on my mom. You're disgusting and a disgrace to the ministry. Wait until my dad hears what you said to my mom. You hypocrite!" I left, slamming the door behind me. Mom came running behind me. She caught me before I got to the house and said, "Let me handle this. Your father already doesn't like this guy, so let's not add to the situation by telling him what you overheard. If you don't want him to preside at your wedding, no problem. I wouldn't do it, and I'm sure your father wouldn't have a problem with it either." So I didn't tell Dad right then.

While we were walking home from church, I asked Mom if she was going to tell Dad what had happened. She said, "Yes. I'm not going to let that man get away with disrespecting me and our family. Your dad won't like what he did. Plus, he doesn't like him anyway and has good reason not to." After Dad said grace at the dinner table that evening, Mom told Dad what had happened. The look on his face said it all. Dad was not happy. He said, "I'm not surprised. That son of a gun is a scoundrel. I'll have a talk with him."

The following Sunday, Dad came to the church when he knew the worship service was over and went straight to the pastor's office. When the pastor saw Dad, he said, "Haven't seen you in awhile, Mr. Stearnes. What can I help you with?" Dad said, "We need to talk." The pastor invited him into his office and closed the door. Mom, Joyce and I were outside the door trying to listen, but we couldn't hear anything. When the door opened five minutes later, Dad and the pastor shook hands. Then Dad said, "Come on, ladies, let's go home." I don't know what Dad said, but he certainly made an impression on that pastor. From then on, the pastor had very little to say to Mom and treated her and the rest of our family with the utmost respect.

A few months later, I told Dad the pastor was asked to leave the church. Dad was happy about that. He said, "Good. The church is doing the right thing. That man is not good for the church or anything else." EF Hutton had spoken.

Besides our church activities, we also had time to enjoy social events. Joyce and I loved to party, and so did our friends. Parents in our neighborhood would schedule parties on Fridays, never on Saturdays or Sundays. Saturday was the day for household chores, shopping and Bible study. Sunday was for church, sometimes all day. We called the parties "house parties" because whoever had a house large enough to accommodate at least 30 kids and some of their parents would sponsor the party. Admission was usually $.50 or $1.00 to cover expenses for the food.

Dad or Mom would escort us to the party. We were not allowed to go if one of them wasn't with us. Mom went most of the time. When she went, Dad would walk with the three of us to the party and would come back and pick us up when Mom called. He felt his family was safer that way. The parties were in the basement of the homes, and the parents would be upstairs doing whatever parents do. But Mom wouldn't stay upstairs. She would come down to the basement and party with us. We didn't want her there, but we had no choice. She could get away with this because the kids who didn't know her thought she was our big sister. We would not say a word. Some of the guys, thinking that Mom was our older sister, would try to sweet-talk her.

Fans Called Him "Turkey," I Called Him Dad

Mom would brush them off, in a nice way, unless they got mannish. Then she would let them know who she was. The looks on their faces were worth our weight in gold. To avoid incidents like this, we would try to convince Dad to stay at the party instead of Mom. He wouldn't. Dad wasn't into parties. He would walk us there, leave and come back to pick us up promptly at Mom's appointed time. Either way, we had fun and were happy to have Dad escort us home.

In our west side neighborhood, there were several black-owned businesses. All of them were within walking distance of our home. Two of our favorites were the movie theater and the bowling alley. Whenever kids talked about going to see a movie, they said "show," not "movie." Once the chores were done and Bible study was over, Saturday was our day to go to the show or the bowling alley. If we decided to go to the show, Dad would walk with us there, drop us off and pick us up when the movie ended. The guys didn't like it. For obvious reasons, they wanted to walk us home, but we felt better and safer walking with Dad. We were tomboys and weren't thinking about the guys. The only thing we wanted them to do was spend their money on us once we got inside.

If we chose to go bowling, Dad would do the same thing. He walked us to the bowling alley, gave us money to pay for refreshments and whatever we needed, and then left. We would call home when we finished bowling, and Dad would come back to walk us home. Those were some of the benefits having Dad escort us places. Most of the time, Mom would go with us because she liked to bowl. If one of our neighbors wanted to join us and had a car, we'd get a ride. Before we decided what we were going to do on Saturdays, though, Mom had to check with Dad to make sure we weren't interfering with his baseball schedule. Dad was adamant about going to all of the Tigers' home games. He was one of their best fans.

Mom and Dad imposed house rules, and one of these was for the daily chores. They worked out the schedule together. The chores were rotated. One week I would have the downstairs, and Joyce would have the upstairs. Whoever had the downstairs had to do the dishes and to clean the living room, dining room, family room and kitchen.

Whoever had the upstairs had to clean the bathroom, hallway, steps and four bedrooms. Mom, Joyce and I did the laundry, helped with the cooking and fed the dog. The next week, Joyce and I switched. When we didn't do what we were supposed to do, we were punished according to the severity of our actions. Dad wouldn't spank us but, boy, would come up with some crazy things for us to do. Some of our punishments would be no television for a week, no playing games. In the summertime, he would punish us by not letting us go outside for two or three days and not letting us play baseball for two or three days. Dad would give us a choice: spanking or other punishment. We would opt for the spanking because the sting would last only for a few minutes and would be over and done with. Mom wouldn't give us a choice. She always made the final decision.

Dad would lay down the law when Joyce and I went partying. Mom supported him in this. When we were teenagers, we had to be home by midnight. When we were younger, we had to be on the front porch before the streetlights came on. I saw Dad dance only a few times, so I don't know if he could or not. Mom was a good dancer and even started a club for Joyce and me so that we could keep up with the latest dances. I saw Mom and Dad dancing together only a couple of times, once on his birthday and once on hers. Both times it was in the confines of the living room. Dad would sing or hum the songs that the three of us were dancing to, but he didn't join in.

Holidays are always a good time for our family to be together and celebrate. Our family favorites were Mother's Day, Father's Day, Thanksgiving and Christmas. As children, Joyce and I also liked Halloween. We would dress up in costumes that Mom had made and would go trick-or-treating around the neighborhood. Mom was a great cook and enjoyed cooking for all of the holidays.

Every Halloween, Mom would trick Dad. She knew Dad loved sweet potato pies. She would buy a large pumpkin and carve it, then use the inside to make pumpkin pies. She would make two pies for Dad and two for us. She would make the pumpkin pies look exactly like sweet potato pies. If you weren't careful or hadn't eaten enough sweet potato pies to tell the difference, you wouldn't know. Dad liked to take his two pies to his room so he could eat them without being disturbed and have enough to enjoy later. He knew that if he left them in the kitchen, they would be gone because we would invite our friends and neighbors over and share with them. Everybody loved Mom's cooking.

After Mom had baked the pies, she would set them on the kitchen table to cool. Then she would wait to see what happened. Joyce and I usually got to the kitchen first, and when we saw the pies, we would have trouble figuring out if they were sweet potato or pumpkin. I would say, "Joyce, what do you think?" She would say, "Mom is trying to fool us again. Let's take a little taste." So we would pinch a little bit off one of the pies, and then we knew. The color is the same, but pumpkin pies do not taste quite like sweet potato pies.

Then we would wait for Dad to come in. The three of us would be sitting in the living room watching TV, and Mom would have a little smirk on her face. Dad would go into the kitchen, see the four pies and take two of them up to his room. This usually happened after Dad returned from his evening walk. A few moments later, Dad would come running down the stairs with the pies in his hand, a chunk taken out of one of them, and say, "Nettie Mae, what is this? These are not sweet potato pies. You did it again!" We would be so tickled that we couldn't say anything. Then Dad would slam the pies down on the table, and, if there were any left, he would grab one of the sweet potato pies. He would tell us he didn't see anything funny and storm up the stairs to his room. That was hilarious. What made it so funny was that Mom would do this to him every Halloween. He fell for it every time.

At Christmastime, Dad was a gem at assisting me in putting up the Christmas lights. He would always help me decorate the outside of the house by holding the ladder for me to make sure I wouldn't fall or get hurt while putting up the lights. All the while, he would fuss and tell me that girls shouldn't be climbing on ladders and doing outside work on the house. I would ignore the comments and tell him that someone had to do it. Most of our neighbors were doing it; we didn't want to be left out. Plus, I enjoyed putting up the lights and making designs with them. Dad never knew what design I had in mind, but he was right there to help every time I needed him. He was afraid of heights, so he wouldn't get up on the ladder. Dad's family had a lot of secrets, and I think this was one of them. I always got the feeling that something had happened in Dad's childhood that made him fear heights, but no one ever talked about it.

Going to Chicago to visit family was a must part of our lives. Mom, Joyce and I made a lot of trips to Chicago. We had several relatives there. They wouldn't come to us, so we went to them. Dad would help us pack and give us what we needed for the trip but would stay at home. He said that someone needed to be at the house for safety. Normally, we would take the train, but on occasion, we would ride on a Greyhound bus. We tried many times to convince Dad that he should go with us, but he refused. He was set in his ways and stood his ground, but he did support us and always wanted us to have a good time.

On our return from one particular trip, we caught a cab at the bus station to take us home. When the cab rounded the corner of our street, on Carter, something got our immediate attention. The poles on the porch of the house in the middle of the block were a bright, ugly yellow. You couldn't miss it. Mom said, "Who in their right minds would paint a house that color?" Guess what? It was our house.

Before we had left for Chicago, Mom had told Dad that she wanted him to paint the trim on the porch and around the house. Her mistake was not telling him what color. She assumed he was going to paint it white. She was partly right. When the cab stopped in front of our house, Mom gasped. Joyce and I laughed. Mom was so upset that she hurried out of the cab and ran up onto the porch. Dad heard the cab pull up and came out to help with the luggage, but Mom stopped him in his tracks. She said, "Turk, why did you paint the poles on the porch this color? You can see this a mile away. When I first saw this color, I just knew it was someone else's house, not ours. What were you thinking?" Joyce and I were cracking up but quietly because we didn't want to get slapped.

Dad said, "I wanted to surprise you. You had been complaining that the porch and trim needed painting, so I thought now was a good time while you were in Chicago. But what had happened was I started

---

63

with the white paint and saw at the last minute that I didn't have enough white. So, I went down to the basement and found several cans of the yellow paint. I mixed it all together so that I would have enough to paint the porch like you asked." Mom didn't know what to say. She knew that he had good intentions. It just didn't come out right. She gave him a hug and a kiss and said, "Thanks, honey. Come on, girls, let's get dinner ready." Dad got our luggage, took it up to the bedrooms and went for his usual walk.

While he was gone, Mom told us that we were going to repaint the porch white the next day while Dad was at work. We said, "Mom, Dad was trying to help." She said, "I know. I appreciate the effort, and I loved that he wanted to surprise me, but I can't let that color stay up there another day." Joyce and I thought it was hilarious. We understood what Dad was trying to do, and we loved him for it. We tried to talk Mom into waiting a little while before she painted over it because of all the work Dad had done, but to no avail. She understood, but that loud, ugly yellow got the best of her. The next day, we bought white paint and painted the trim on the porch.

Because my mother was the educator in the family, Dad let her handle all of the business matters, especially when it came to talking to people about contracts and the like. He always felt that she was better able to handle those types of things than he was. It wasn't that he couldn't do it; he just didn't want to. Dad had her back, and she had his. He provided the money; she wrote the checks. They complemented each other. Dad was quiet and conservative. Mom was outgoing and aggressive. Opposites attract, right?

One summer Mom and Dad decided to buy new windows for the living room and the dining room. After seeing advertisements on television for the Belvedere Construction Company, they made an appointment to have a salesman come and give them an estimate. Joyce and I were sitting on the front porch when the salesman arrived. Dad came to the door and let him in. While they were shaking hands, Dad said, "Let's have a seat at the dining room table." The salesman asked a few questions and then opened his book to show Dad some samples. At that point, Dad paused for a moment and called for my mom. He said, "Nettie Mae, come down here for a minute. I want you to look at something."

Mom came down from upstairs and sat next to Dad to look at the samples. Then the salesman asked, "Well, did you see anything you liked?" Dad turned to Mom and said, "Nettie Mae, what do you want to do?" Mom said, "The samples are nice; and everything looks good, but we just wanted an estimate. We need to look around so we can compare prices and get the best deal." Since the salesman had never introduced himself, Mom and Dad thought that he was just a regular salesman. After Mom made her comment, the salesman slammed his sample book shut and asked Dad, "Are you going to let this woman tell you what to do?" Dad said calmly, "My wife makes the final decision. Nettie Mae, what do you want to do?" Mom said, "We're not going to make a decision right now. When I called and made the appointment, I said that all we wanted was an estimate. That's it." The salesman jumped from his seat, hurriedly walked to the door and slammed the screen door on his way out. He slammed it so hard, we thought he had broken it. When he stormed past Joyce and me on the porch, we went into the house and asked, "Who was that? He was so rude!" Mom said, "I don't know, but we're not doing business with him. I have a good mind to call the company and report him." His actions led us to believe that he was a male chauvinist. Later that evening, while we were watching TV, we saw this same guy on the Belvedere commercial. He was the owner of the company, Mr. Belvedere himself. We had an incredibly good laugh.

VII

Education

As far back as I can remember, Dad and Mom impressed upon us the importance of education and were examples for us to follow.

Joyce and I both graduated from elementary school, junior high and high school with honors at the top of our classes. In elementary school, Joyce was double promoted. I wasn't double promoted because Mom thought that it would not be a good idea for me to skip from the 5th grade to the 7th grade. In junior high school, we both were valedictorians of our graduating classes and both won the American Legion Award, which was a top award for an 8th grader. We attended Cass Technical High School, one of the top high schools in Detroit. I graduated in June 1964, and Joyce graduated the following January.

In the fall of 1964, I enrolled at Knoxville College in Knoxville, Tennessee, as a music major. I stayed there only for a semester because the school did not meet my expectations. Mom had wanted me there because one of her brothers, William Henry McArthur, was a professor there. We called him Uncle Bill. She was hoping that he could influence me to stay, but it didn't work. Uncle Bill was head of the biology department and tried to get me to switch majors, but he didn't appreciate my passion for music.

After high school, Joyce attended Eastern Michigan University in Ypsilanti. Both of us wanted to continue our college education, but our lives were about to take a different turn as we began to raise families of our own.

It took a few years for us to get our family lives straightened out to a point where we could resume our college education. Sound familiar?

Now that I think about it, Dad's situation was similar to ours. Like father, like daughters. Several years later, I graduated from Madonna University with a bachelor's degree in business administration and a minor in music. I then earned my master's degree in public administration from Central Michigan University in Mt. Pleasant, with a

My graduation picture from Central Michigan University, 1998.

minor in music. Meanwhile, Joyce earned both her bachelor's and master's degrees from Wayne State University in Detroit. Her bachelor's degree is in education and her master's is in education in administration. This led to her career teaching deaf and hard of hearing students.

So Dad achieved his educational goals despite interruptions, and so did we. We made Dad and Mom proud. We thank God for their unwavering support, encouragement and love throughout our educational journey and for being the examples we and our children and grandchildren needed. The legacy continues.

VIII

Commonalities: Marriage and Divorce

When it comes to marriage, Dad and I also had similar experiences. Dad and I both are divorcees. Dad divorced his first wife for some unknown reason, but, fortunately for Joyce and me, the divorce didn't have a negative effect and he met and married Mom. I'm not sure what prompted his divorce, but I am so glad he married Mom. Mom and Dad were blessed with two daughters. They stayed married for a memorable 33 years before he passed away. Unfortunately, my marriage was just the opposite.

Let me tell you how my ex-husband, James Lee Brown, Jr., and I ended up together in a marriage that lasted 10 rocky years. Our families became neighbors when we moved into the house at 2689 Carter in 1953. His family moved three houses down, going towards Linwood on the opposite side of the street. We lived on the odd side of the street, and they lived on the even.

James wasn't interested in playing baseball with us or the other kids in the neighborhood. His only sports interest was in horses. He and I played chess and checkers together mostly, at Mom's insistence. He was typically a loner and didn't try to fit in with the rest of our crowd. Dad supported Mom in her decision and took the initiative in forcing me to play chess and checkers with James after he broke his left leg in an accident at the riding stables on Belle Isle. The other kids on the block wouldn't play with James. This is when we found out about his love for horses. Aside from Dad and Mom's prodding, I had no interest in James, especially since he had no interest whatsoever in baseball or most other sports. From outward appearances, we had absolutely nothing in common.

My attitude changed after James was discharged from his tour of duty as a communications specialist in the United States Army in the summer of 1964. Like most young women my age, I was attracted to a man in a uniform. Something about a man in a uniform sent chills down my spine. It wasn't long after his return home from the military that James and I started dating. Our relationship developed into a love relationship.

The birth of my son, Tony, on August 19, 1968, on our front porch was nothing short of a miracle. It would have gone viral if there had been social media. We didn't make it to the hospital in time. My dad and my mom tried their best to get me to Dad's car, but it was too late. Everyone was expecting my son to be born in October. I had been praying for him to come earlier than October so that I could go back to college in September. My prayers were answered. Be careful what you pray for. Not only was my son born prematurely, but because I wasn't totally prepared for what I had prayed for, he was born on the front porch of our home on Carter. It was unexpected but a pleasant surprise. After his birth on the front porch, my family and some of my neighbors were running around like chickens with their heads cut off. Just like in the movies. No one was getting anything done. It was hilarious.

After a few hours, despite all the chaos, the police finally arrived and took me with Dad to Harper Hospital. My pediatrician, Dr. Foster, was in shock. So was Dad. Dr. Foster and several nurses met us at the hospital door with a bed. After the initial shock wore off, during the next week Dad came to the hospital every day. When he came to visit, Dad would sit and watch TV with me for a little while and leave a bag of fruit that he always brought. On the second day, he walked into my room and I said, "Dad, guess what I named my son?" He said, "What?" I said, "Norman Anthony Brown. Since you don't have any sons, I named him Norman after you." He said, with a smile on his face, "Ooh, that's a classic." The smile on his face said it all. Dad was happy that he finally had a namesake.

That same day, a few hours after he had left, I got a call from Mom. She asked me if Dad had come to the hospital. I said, "Yes, he left a few hours ago." She said, "Well, did he say where he was going?" I said, "No, I thought that he was going home." She said, "Oh, my goodness. This is not like your dad. Where could he be?" I said, "Check with the guys at the barber shop. He might be there." She said, "I'll call you back later when we find him."

I was a little worried. Dad always followed the same routine. While I was in the hospital, he always came at noon. He would bring a small bag of fruit that I gave away to the nurses. The first time he brought the fruit, I put the bag into a drawer. The next day, when I opened the drawer, there were fruit flies in it. That was a mess. From then on until I left the hospital, unbeknownst to Dad, I gave the fruit away. I didn't want to hurt his feelings by telling him not to bring it, so I took it, gave him a kiss and gave it away after he left. He never knew.

I tried to think where Dad could have gone. I figured that he must have walked home because if he had taken the bus, he would have been home by now. The more I thought about it, the more worried I got.

After another hour, Mom finally called and said, "Guess where I found your dad?" I said, "Where?" She said, "I walked up to the barber shop, and there he was, passing out cigars." She said Dad was so happy to have a namesake that he had walked to the store down the street from the hospital, bought a box of cigars and passed them out to everyone he met on the street on his way home. He told everyone, "My daughter just had a baby boy, and she named him Norman, after me." That was a 15-mile walk. Dad walked from Harper Hospital on John R and Mack to the barber shop on Linwood and Euclid. He didn't even break a sweat.

When he came to the hospital the next day, he brought my favorites: a chocolate ice cream cone, a bag of chips and a bottle of Faygo Rock & Rye. Lunch was extra special that day. Dad finally had a namesake, and I was glad to do that for him. James wasn't too happy about it, though. He wanted me to name my son after him, James Lee Brown, Jr. My son's name would be James Lee Brown III. I wanted my son to have a more profound name. I put my foot down and said, "There is no way I'm going to name my son James Lee Brown anything. There are already too many James Browns in the world, plus Norman is a classic." James liked Anthony but not Norman, but it wasn't up to him. I had done all the work. He was just the sperm donor. Dad was happy, and that was good enough for me.

A week later, I returned home from the hospital. Because our son, Tony, was born two months earlier than expected, he had to stay in the premature nursery at the hospital for another week. While he was there, James and I continued with our original plans to get married the first week in October. In spite of our planning, we weren't prepared for what happened next.

What should have been one of the happiest days of my life almost turned into a fiasco. Every girl dreams about her wedding day, and I was no different. Saturday, October 12, 1968, was the big day. James and I would exchange vows, and I would become Mrs. Brown in a ceremony at his grandmother's home with just the immediate family from both sides present. But the wedding almost didn't take place. First, Mom and my sister decided they weren't coming. They didn't like James and decided to go to Chicago, hoping that would deter or postpone the wedding. *Not!* Dad was the only member of my family who planned to attend. Then, on the day of the wedding, Dad was filling in for someone at the laundromat on the corner of our street. How he could forget that I was getting married, I'll never know, but it should have been an omen for me.

When we got to James' grandmother's home, everyone else who had been invited to come was there except Dad. I immediately announced, "There will be no wedding without my dad." Everybody, especially my fiancé, looked at me as if I were crazy. I handed my bouquet to my fiancé and told him that I was going to find my dad and bring him to the ceremony. Everyone would just have to wait until I got back. We both left and went looking for my dad. Our guests were appalled.

We drove to my dad's house, and he wasn't there. I went out on the porch and was trying to figure out where he could be. While I was standing there, one of my neighbors asked me what was wrong. I said,

"I'm looking for my dad." He said, "Your dad is up at the laundromat, working. One of the guys didn't show up." I said, "Thanks. You're a life-saver." James was waiting for me in the car. I ran to the car and said, "James, let's go. Dad is at the laundromat."

When we got to the laundromat, I didn't even wait for James to stop. I opened the door, ran into the laundromat, saw my dad and said, "Dad, what are you doing? Today is my wedding day, and you are sup-posed to be giving me away!" Dad saw the tears in my eyes and imme-diately stopped what he was doing. Then he got on the phone and called for someone to take his place. He didn't explain. He just said that he had an emergency and had to leave. He knew how important this was to me, and I could tell from the expression on his face that he had forgotten. He was going to make this right.

After he got off the phone, he said, "Come on, Pretty Girl. I have to go home and change clothes. You know I wouldn't miss your wed-ding for anything in the world." He grabbed my hand and we both ran out of the back door, down the alley and to our house. When we got there, Dad ran up the stairs from the living room, freshened up in the bathroom and changed his clothes. While he was getting ready, I ran back to the laundromat and got James, who was waiting in the car in front of the laundromat for us to come out. I told him, "Drive back to the house. Dad should be ready when we get there. I'll tell you later what happened."

Sure enough, when we got back to the house, Dad was standing on the front porch patiently waiting for us, dressed in his Sunday best. He looked good, and now we both felt good. Dad was ready for my wedding. When we arrived at James' grandmother's home, everyone breathed a sigh of relief. A few comments were made, and then Gail, his sister, said, "Okay, everyone. They're back. Let's get this show on the road." The ceremony had a rocky start, but once Dad was there, everything else fell into place.

After our marriage, I always could count on Dad to help wher-ever and whenever I needed him. Whether it was helping around the house, babysitting or providing emotional support, he was a great dad and granddad.

Having a father who loved my sister and me unconditionally and was very supportive and nonjudgmental makes living so much more worthwhile. Dad was just this type of person. When I finally decided to get a divorce, Dad was supportive through the whole process and had no fear. He kept it moving in a positive manner and without chastisement.

While we were dating, James was the perfect gentleman, but his behavior gradually changed after our marriage. Several incidents occurred that supported my eventual decision to get a divorce. The first one happened two years after we were married, when James and I were living in a basement apartment near the corner of Chicago and Dexter, eight blocks from Mom and Dad. One night I came home and started cooking dinner when I heard a voice say, "Stop cooking, and go get your son." That had to be the voice of God giving me a warning because there was no one near me who could have said it. Some people would find that hard to believe, but I believed it. I listened to the voice and immediately stopped cooking.

While I was walking to get Tony from the bedroom, I heard another voice say, "Duck!" I listened to the voice again, and I ducked. Just then, I felt a blast of wind swoosh past my head. It was James' fist. While I was bent over, I was near my coffee table, so I picked it up, turned around and hit my husband over the head with it. I hit him so hard that I knocked him out and broke the coffee table. Then I decided I had better get out of there quickly. I ran barefoot out to the street in the snow and flagged down a cab. I gave the cab driver my dad's address and told him to please hurry.

When the cab pulled in front of my dad's house, I jumped out, told the driver to wait and ran to the door, calling for Dad. When I got to the door, Dad opened it and said, "Pretty Girl, what's wrong?" I said, "Dad, you have to go back to the apartment with me to get my son. James wants to fight. I'll explain everything later. We have to go." Dad said, "Okay, let's go." While Dad was walking out of the door, I ran to the closet and got my baseball bat. Mom came down the stairs to find out what all of the commotion was about. I said, "I'm in a hurry. I'll tell you later when we get back." When I came out of the closet with the baseball bat, Dad said, "What are you going to do with that?" I said, "If James gets past you, he's going to run into this."

We ran out of the house and got into the cab, leaving Mom standing at the door, wondering. When we got back to my apartment building, Dad paid the cab driver and told me to stay behind him while he opened the door to my apartment. When he opened the door, we could see that James was just picking himself up off the floor. He looked at my dad and said, "Mr. Stearnes, your daughter is strong as a bull. While I was in the army, I was hit with blackjacks and rifles, but your daughter hit me one time and I saw stars." Dad said, "As long as I live, don't you ever put your hands on my daughter." Then Dad looked at me and said, "Get your son, and let's go. I'll keep an eye on James."

While Dad watched my husband, I went to the bedroom and packed our belongings. Meanwhile, James was talking to Dad and trying to figure out what I was going to do next. When I came out of the bedroom after packing, James said, "What are you doing?" I said, "I'm leaving. That's why I went and got Dad." James just stood there with a dumb look on his face. He was still a little groggy. I picked up my son. Then Dad and I left with Tony. When we got outside, Dad flagged a cab and we went to my parents' home. Mom had been patiently waiting to hear what had happened. Dad explained while I put my son to bed. When I was done, Mom told me, "Good thing I wasn't there. He deserved to be knocked out. Don't worry. You can stay as long as you need to. I hope you knocked some sense into James."

I stayed for six months. During those six months, Mom convinced me to go back to James because she didn't believe in divorce and thought that we could work things out. James was on his best behavior for the whole time and made a good impression on Mom. Dad wasn't impressed. I had my doubts, but I trusted Mom, so I went back. This was the beginning of several other incidents involving James becoming increasingly violent without provocation toward me during the course of our marriage, eventually ending in divorce. Through it all, Dad was there whenever I needed him. Thank God for dads like him.

The Great Babysitter

Taking on the dual role of dad and granddad is no easy task. Some men step up to the plate while others stay in the dugout. When Joyce and I had children of our own, Dad readily accepted the challenge. He became our main babysitter and enjoyed every minute of it. My sister and I worked every morning, so we would drop the kids off before 8:00 a.m. My sister had twin sons and a daughter, and I had a son. Her daughter, Karen, was two years older than her brothers and my son. They were close. They did everything together, and my dad got a kick out of it. Dad never had any sons, so he was totally loving having three grandsons.

Every morning, after we dropped the kids off, Dad would take them with him on a bus ride to downtown Detroit. When they got off the bus, they would go to the Awrey's bakery, where Dad would buy goodies for them (cakes, pies, doughnuts, etc.). Then they would walk around downtown, eating and playing. After the walk, they would go back to the bus stop and feed the pigeons and other birds while they waited for the bus. When the bus arrived, they would get on it and go home. Dad would do this every day during the week, weather permitting, and our children loved it.

One day the children had been giving my mother a lot of trouble, so she made them stay in their rooms and wait for us to come home. This was not normal. Usually, my mom would engage them in some type of activity until my sister and I got home and she would feed them. Mom was a great cook. I knew something was wrong because when I walked through the door, I didn't hear any noise and didn't see the kids. Mom was sitting in the living room chair and watching television. Curiosity got the best of me, so I said, "Mom, what's going on?" She said, "You and your sister dropped the kids off five minutes late, so your dad left them. They cried and were misbehaving all day long. They were mad that their granddaddy left them." Lesson learned. My dad was a stickler for doing things on time. From then on, I was never late. I dropped my son off every day *before* 8:00 a.m. so that my son would not get left. My sister tried. Most of the time she made it, but sometimes she didn't. Then, of course, my mom would suffer the consequences. Those were the good old days.

On one particular bus trip, Dad and the kids were standing at the bus stop, waiting for the bus as usual. When the bus pulled in front of them, one of the ladies in the back of the bus looked out the window and said, "Look at those little motley kids. I wonder who they belong to and why their parents didn't clean their faces." After Dad and our kids got on the bus and started walking towards their seats, she gasped, "Oh, my God. I know those kids. One of them is mine, and the other three must be his cousins! They can't go downtown looking like a motley crew. That's embarrassing!" My son recognized her, but his cousins didn't. Tony said, "Hey, Grandma." The woman turned out to be my husband's grandmother. She took Tony by the hand, made him sit down next to her and pulled out her handkerchief. She wet the handkerchief with water from her thermos and wiped his face. She did the same thing for his three cousins.

Then she scolded my dad. "Mr. Stearnes, you tell Rosilyn and Joyce that the next time I see these kids on the bus, their faces better be clean. Don't let these kids come out of the house looking like that. I was talking about these kids and didn't realize that one of them was mine until they got on the bus. I had to swallow my tongue." Dad explained that normally Mom would have checked them before they left the house, but he had to grab the kids and hurry to the bus stop to keep from missing the bus. He assured her that it wouldn't happen again. Later that evening, when Joyce and I came to pick up our kids, Dad and Mom told us what had happened and read us the riot act. We didn't make that mistake again.

At the corner of our block on Carter and Linwood was a small grocery store owned by Mr. and Mrs. Rankin. The Rankins were genuinely nice people and assets to the community. They contributed to many community activities and provided services such as cashing personal checks and hiring teenagers during the summer to work in their store.

One school day, while Joyce and I were at work, our children came home from school for lunch and found no one there and the doors locked. Dad and Mom had forgotten that my son and Joyce's three children were due home at lunchtime. Dad was working at the laundromat, and Mom was running errands. Our children didn't know what else to do, so they walked to the Rankins' store at the corner of Linwood and Carter. When Mrs. Rankin saw that they were by themselves, she asked why and whether they were supposed to be in school. They said they were hungry and came home for lunch, but no one was there. Mr. Rankin came from behind the counter with four crates and sat our children on the crates. Then the Rankins fed our children. After they finished eating, Mr. Rankin escorted our kids back to school.

That evening, when Dad came to the store to purchase his usual goodies, Mrs. Rankin told him what had happened. Dad thanked the Rankins for what they had done and reimbursed them for feeding his grandchildren. Mr. Rankin told Dad he wasn't worried about being reimbursed because he knew Dad would take care of business. That was the kind of relationship and respect the Rankins and Dad had for each other, and they loved our kids.

In 1973, five years after the birth of our son, Tony, my husband finally got a chance to do something that he absolutely loved—be a cowboy. My husband loved horses and got his training from the man who was the owner of the riding stable on Belle Isle. He trained my husband in every aspect of the business, and this became my husband's first love. No one really knew how good he was until he got the opportunity to manage a riding stable in South Lyon, Michigan, called Green Acres. The owner of Green Acres had terminal cancer and needed someone to take over the business, so he called my husband and, of course, James said yes. This was a dream come true for him. We moved to South Lyon, James, our son and I. This broke some of the stereotypes that people have about black families. We were the only black family in South Lyon and the only black family managing a riding stable in that area.

When I told my parents we were moving to South Lyon to manage a riding stable, they had mixed emotions. Mom was shocked because she remembered James as a kid who lived across the street when I was growing up. She had no clue that he had any experience with horses. Dad was just happy that we were moving to a place of our own. I think in his own way he was trying to tell me something. After we got settled, we gave our family and friends an open invitation. We wanted everyone to share in our new adventure. My dad was all for it. When he came to visit, he would bring the entire Stearnes family. This included my mom, my sister and her three children; they would come on the weekends. Coming out to the riding stable was an enjoyable and fun event for the kids and gave Mom and Dad a welcome break.

My mom didn't particularly like horses because she had had a frightful experience as a teenager. She had been in a field, walking home from school. There were horses grazing in the field. While she was walking, trying to get to the other side of the field, one of the horses stopped grazing, looked at her and started running towards her. Mom thought he was going to harm her, so she took off running. She managed to get to the fence and to jump over it before he could reach her. She ran all the way home. She never understood why the horse had chased her. That made a lasting impression on her, one that she would never forget. She said it was one of the scariest moments of her life.

When she and my dad would come to the stables, she would keep her distance from the horses. One time she was standing up against a fence and didn't realize that a horse was standing behind her. The horse slowly got closer to the part of the fence where she was standing and put his head over the fence and sneezed. That startled my mom. She thought the horse was trying to bite her. She jumped away from the fence and yelled, "Roz, come get this horse. He's trying to bite me!" She was really scared. I came over, hugged my mom and explained that the horse was only sneezing and wanted to be petted. That's why he had put his head over the fence. I tried to get her to go back to the fence and to put her hand on his head and just to stroke him, but the sneeze was enough for her. She was afraid to go back, so I didn't force her to do it.

After several trips to the stable, Mom finally came around and realized that horses are in many ways just like people. They need love, too. Dad was quite the opposite. He loved being at the stables and being in the country, especially with our children. Dad was a country boy at heart. After he saw how well my son, Tony, and James could ride, he gave my son a nickname—"Cowboy." After that, whenever he saw my son, he would call him "Cowboy." My son loved that. The nickname stuck until Dad died. My son and my husband won many awards at horse shows for their riding prowess. Both won first place at the Michigan State Fair in 1979, riding in the Appaloosa competition. They made my dad proud.

My son, Tony, on his pony, Mercy, at the Michigan State Fair Horse Competition in Detroit, 1976.

Both James and I had entered into our marriage with our promise of being together for the rest of our lives. Little did we know that it would end in divorce. Love is blind, and what you think is love just may not be. In my situation, this proved to be true. I had married James Lee Brown, Jr., despite my mom's and sister's objections. I had thought they were just being obstinate, and I had wanted to prove them wrong. I had believed true love conquers all. To this day, I still believe that.

After 10 years of marriage, I had to eat crow. James had proven my mother and sister right. Although we had married for love and had wanted to raise a family in what I believed was the right way, James turned out to be someone with whom I could not live. After a few separations and many discussions and efforts to try to make my marriage work, all my efforts were in vain. I eventually had to file for divorce, and the events leading up to finalization of the divorce would fill another book. My husband's behavior had become increasingly bizarre and abusive.

When Dad and I were talking about problems that had led to my divorce, to ease my apprehension and dismay, he took me in his arms and calmly said, "I never liked the guy anyway." Dad is the one person about whom I can say, "He never had a bad word to say about anybody. Never." So when he made that comment about James, it really hit home. I was furious. I said, "Dad, if you had told me that before I married him, I never would have gotten married." But I knew in my heart Dad was trying not to interfere.

My dad didn't have a spiteful bone in his body, and if he had said those words, even if he had said them at the wedding, there would not have been a wedding. I would have known that my dad saw something in James that wasn't right. I would have grabbed my dad's arm, walked out and left James standing at the altar. I would have dealt with the consequences later.

IX

Twice Retired:
Dad and Me

Both Dad and I lived long enough to retire not once but twice. We could be proud of that. One retirement was from a profession that we absolutely loved, and the other was from a job of necessity because our families needed our support. Our work habits were similar, too. Baseball was Dad's passion. Dad's first retirement was from the National Negro Leagues in 1945, after a long and phenomenally successful 25-year career that led to his induction into the Baseball Hall of Fame 58 years later. After his retirement from baseball, he went to work for Ford Motor Company, where he retired for the second time after 27 years. At that time, since he realized that his dream of playing in the major leagues would not become a reality now because of his age, he did what a real man would do: get a job.

The amazing thing about this was that he worked in a place that tested not only his physical strength and power but also his morality and the strength of his character. Dad excelled in that as well. I don't know how he did it, but he did.

I was hired in 1968 at Michigan Bell Telephone Company and retired from there in 1995 after 27 years. By then the company was known as Ameritech. Dad worked for a total of 49 years at his two jobs, and I worked for a total of 40 years at my two. Put all of that together for a combined total of 89 years. All I can say is, "Wow! Thank God."

I started work at Michigan Bell Telephone Company after my son was born. I started as a clerk in White Pages, was promoted to supervisor and 10 years later was assigned to the residential department. I retired seven years after that in 1995. While at Michigan Bell, I was active in unionizing the workforce at the company in the Communications Workers of America union and I was elected our union's first president. I learned a lot about the corporate world at Ameritech and developed lifetime relationships there, but that job was not my first love. In 1998, I went to work for the Detroit Public Schools as an accompanist/teacher at Edward Duke Ellington Conservatory of Music & Art. That was my forte and my passion for the next 13 fun-filled years until I retired for the second time in 2011. It was years before I realized how fortunate and blessed Dad and I had been to have these same types of experiences. "Like father, like daughter."

When Dad retired from Ford in 1964, he suffered some hearing loss because of the conditions that he had worked in. Despite his hearing loss, Dad wouldn't wear hearing aids. He didn't like all of the things that he heard when he was wearing them. It was too much for him. Nowadays, such working conditions would have been grounds for a lawsuit. But did he sue? *No.* That was never an issue. My mom didn't think about that either. So what do we call that? Humility, dedication, selflessness. What? I call it just being grateful for the things that you have and not being greedy. That's another reason why I so loved and honored both of my parents. They weren't greedy or selfish and treated people the way they wanted to be treated.

During his second retirement, Dad became one of the best Detroit Tigers fans ever, if not *the* best. He would go to every Tigers home game and sit in the bleachers. I thought Dad just didn't want to pay for a more expensive seat, so I paid for us to go to a game and bought seats behind home plate, which were some of the best seats in the stadium. I went to get refreshments, and when I returned, Dad was gone. I asked some of the men around me where he was, and one of them said, "Your dad said to tell you that he would be in the bleachers." I was like "What?" I went to the bleachers, where, sure enough, there he was, drinking beer and making conversation with the guys around him and thoroughly enjoying himself.

I couldn't be upset because he was so happy. I sat myself down and joined in the fun. Lesson learned. From then on, I bought bleacher tickets and passed the word on to the rest of the family. If we weren't at the games, we always knew if the Tigers were winning or not. If they were losing badly, Dad would leave, come home and listen to the rest of the game on the radio and fuss. If they were winning, he would stay for the entire game and come home with a smile on his face. Whenever we could not find my father at home or at his other favorite spots, we knew exactly where he was: Tiger Stadium.

X

Negro Leagues
Reunion 1979
in Ashland, Kentucky

June and July 1979 were good months for Dad. One morning during the last week of June, my sister had gone into Dad's room and had noticed he had a letter on his dresser. The letter was an invitation to attend a Negro Leagues ballplayers reunion. This was the first of its kind. The reunion was going to be held in Ashland, Kentucky, on the weekend of July 6, 1979. Dad was pleasantly surprised and happy.

My sister was just as surprised and excited as Dad. She told Dad that he needed to attend the reunion so he could see his teammates. Most of these men, like Dad, were in their 70s and 80s or older. Several of their teammates had passed away. He hadn't seen or heard from these guys since he had retired in 1945, except for Satchel Paige and Double Duty Radcliffe. Joyce recalled that Dad was hesitant to attend the reunion at first, but he finally agreed to go. She telephoned Tom Stultz, the host of the event. He told her, even though it was last minute, he "would be honored to have us attend."

Satchel always would come to our house to visit Dad whenever he came to Detroit for an exhibition with the Harlem Globetrotters. He and Dad would sit on the front porch and reminisce. I didn't know it then, but we were listening to Negro Leagues baseball history. We should have taken pictures and recorded some of their conversations. I thought they were just "shooting the breeze." Darn! Anyway, when Dad decided to go to the reunion, Joyce and I knew that we had our work cut out for us. Dad was a homebody and didn't travel very much after he retired from baseball. It was like pulling teeth to get him to travel.

As usual, Dad let my mom, my sister and me do the planning for the trip. I would be responsible for Dad's outfits, and Joyce would accompany him to the reunion. As much as I wanted to go, I couldn't take off work. I was a supervisor at Michigan Bell, and we had deadlines to meet. That meant Joyce and her boyfriend, Chester, would travel with Dad. Dad was just as excited as we were. This was his first reunion, and it promised to be a memorable event. To this day I wish I had gone. I would have been able to meet these great men face to face and to hear their stories. I would have been in the midst of greatness. Mom regretted not going, too. We missed so much. That was the chance of a lifetime. We could have gotten autographs and pictures. Now all of those men have passed, and their stories need to be told.

Taking Dad shopping for the reunion literally wore me out. We went to Northland Mall in Southfield, and our first stop was at Sears. There was a good sale in the men's department. I wanted Dad to have two sports coats, two pairs of pants, two shirts, a suit, a pair of dress shoes, a hat and house shoes. Dad had everything else he needed. I saw the sports coats that I wanted for him, and I knew Dad's size. He was the same size as James. Dad tried to pretend that he wore a larger size because he liked baggy clothes. I think he did this because he was getting older and just wanted to relax.

Either way, throughout the entire shopping spree, we argued. Dad wanted to have his own way, and I wanted to have mine. When I picked out the sports coats, I saw a man following us and grinning. I asked him, "What are you doing?" He asked, "Is that your dad? I've been watching you for a little while, and the two of you are funny." I said, "This is not funny. Would you like to help me?" He said, "Sure, what do you want me to do?" I said, "Go into the dressing room with my dad, and let me know if the clothes fit." He said, "No problem," and he did. That helped. He did the same thing when Dad tried on his suit. Picking out the hat was no problem. Dad picked the hat himself. That was the only time we didn't get into an argument. My helper gave me a thumbs up and left. I didn't even think to get his name. He was a godsend.

Next and last on the list were the shoes. I told Dad, "Your turn. Since we have everything else, go get the shoes you want to match your suit." I was tired. Dad went over to the shoe department, and when he came back, he had a pair of house shoes. I said, "Dad, you can't wear house shoes with your suit. You need dress shoes." He said, "But these are more comfortable. I'm going to be doing a lot of walking." I said, "All right. Keep the house shoes because you'll need them, too, but not to wear with your suit." I had to take Dad back over to the shoe department to get the dress shoes. Then we left the store and headed home. Mom had cooked dinner for us, but I was too tired to eat. I drank some juice, took a bath and went to bed. Dad took his packages up to his room, ate dinner and then went for his usual walk.

Getting Dad ready for the trip to Ashland proved to be a lot of fun but challenging, too. After I got Dad outfitted for the trip, Mom helped Dad pack, and Joyce made the travel arrangements. Joyce and her boyfriend, Chester, were to accompany Dad to Kentucky. When Chester drove up to our house, Mom and I walked with Joyce and Dad to the porch, said our goodbyes and watched as they left for the airport.

This is what my sister remembers about the trip and the reunion:

"We would be flying from Detroit Metropolitan Airport on Delta Airlines Flight 1727 on July 3 to Cincinnati, Ohio, then laying over for four hours in Cincinnati before flying to Ashland, Kentucky.

"Dad had a fear of flying, so I neglected to tell him that we were traveling by plane. Upon arrival at the airport, he asked, 'Why are we stopping here?' I calmly stated, 'We are flying to Cincinnati first, Dad. Then we have to take another plane to Kentucky.' The look on his face was priceless. Then he said, 'Aw, Bugsy.' I know that he was not thrilled about flying, but he went along with my decision because he loved me just like he loved Bugs Bunny. That was a lot.

"At the airport in Cincinnati, the three of us went to a sports bar that had a pool table. Chester and I played pool while Dad watched. When it was time to board the second plane, we had to walk out onto the runway to board a Piedmont Airlines turboprop airplane, Flight

924. I did not know these types of planes were still flying commercially, so I think we were a little nervous at first, especially Dad. The plane had to be started by hand. This was not the sort of thing you would expect to happen in this day and age with the advancements in airplanes.

"Once on board this dinosaur of a plane, Dad looked out his window, and while seeing the white clouds and the beautiful sky from so high up in the airplane, he smiled and said, 'Wow! What man can do!' At that moment it was clear to all of us that his fear of flying had disappeared. Then he started singing one of his favorite songs, 'My Country 'Tis of Thee.'

"Joe Lapointe, a sportswriter for the *Detroit Free Press*, was on the plane along with Hall of Famer Ernie Banks of the Chicago Cubs and a few other persons. Joe struck up a conversation with Dad for a good portion of the trip. That proved to be the beginning of a treasured relationship that is still embraced by our family.

"After we landed, Chester rented a four-door sedan at the airport and drove us to the Holiday Inn in Ashland by way of U.S. Route 52. When we checked in, we noticed that all of the rooms for the Negro Leagues ballplayers were in the same location so they could be close together, but their other guests and family members were in a different part of the hotel. Dad came to my room and said he wanted to be in a room next to Chester and me. Therefore, I went to the hotel receptionist and asked if Dad could be moved to an adjoining room. The receptionist honored my request. Dad also asked us to leave the connecting door to the adjoining rooms open because that made him feel more comfortable. I realized he wasn't used to being away from home, so I did not want him to be filled with anxiety.

"That evening we went to the home of Tom Stultz in Greenup, where the ballplayers and their families had gathered for a birthday party for Negro Leaguer Clint 'The Hawk' Thomas. 'Country' Jake Stephens, another Negro Leaguer, walked up to Dad, shook his hand and said, 'Hey, Turkey! Do you remember me?' Dad looked at him and said, 'Naw.' Dad had a hard time understanding him and the others, too, because he had a hearing loss and refused to wear his hearing aids.

Therefore, the players had to speak in a loud voice, and I had to interpret for him throughout the trip.

"Quincy Trouppe, another of the ballplayers, proved to be quite a character. He told me that he was the only person with film footage of their games, but he did not have any footage of Dad. Then he announced that he had written a book and said, 'I just happen to have a copy of my book with me.' Everyone laughed, but I never saw the book.

"It was amazing to hear the players talk about Dad's outstanding ability to hit, run the bases and field. They complimented him numerous times, and softly he accepted their praise and adoration. Chester and I were in awe to see the poise they had and the love and admiration they had for each other, and to hear their love for the game and to realize that they did not express any bitterness for the racism they had endured or for the obstacles that had been placed in their paths. They were humble just like Dad.

"The next day the ballplayers, sportswriters and I went to the dock to go on a steamboat ride. Chester remained at the hotel. When Dad saw the steamboat, he asked, 'Who's going on a boat?' I responded, 'We are! You'll be fine!'

"While they were boarding the boat, Dad made sure he was the last one in line. No one paid Dad any attention. After the boat crew started down the river, someone said, 'Look, Turkey is on the dock, waving at us. He's supposed to be on the boat.' They turned around and went back to get Dad. All of them had to get off the boat to usher Dad aboard because he said, 'You got my feet off the ground once; you're not going to do that again.' It took some persuading, but they finally got him onto the boat.

"Negro Leaguers Clint Thomas, Monte Irvin, Buck Leonard, Leon Day, Judy Johnson, Gene Benson, Quincy Trouppe, Ted Page and Ray Dandridge were all on the boat. Hall of Famer Bob Feller from the Cleveland Indians and Ernie Banks were seated next to them, and a gentleman with a video camera was standing in back of the players. However, I do not know if there is a video of this event.

"All of the Negro Leagues ballplayers sported dress or casual suits, and they looked fabulous. One of the players said Satchel Paige was ill and unable to attend. They appeared sad and disappointed that Satchel had to miss this engagement. Satchel died three years later.

"Chester and I were afforded the opportunity to have a brief discussion with Ernie Banks, and someone took a picture of us during that conversation. Ernie was very friendly and excited about seeing Dad and the other ballplayers and hearing them talk about their experiences.

"After the boat ride, I noticed that some of the men had baseballs for autograph signing. The baseball was extremely difficult for the players to sign because of its size. I asked Chester to drive me to a store to purchase a softball because it's bigger. Dad went with us and said the sedan was a smooth-riding car and he really liked it. I did not realize at the time that the autographed baseball had the most value, or I would have purchased several. Instead, I gave the autographed baseball to my sister, Rosilyn. I still have the autographed softball with all ten of their signatures. They were happy and eager to sign it because it was easy to write on. Their signatures are still legible, and I have an important piece of history in my possession.

"That night at the banquet there were lots of introductions and speeches. It was a long night. The ballplayers were supposed to sit at the long table prepared for them on the stage above the rest of the attendees. Dad was fine until he saw that Chester and I weren't sitting with him. He got up and sat down where we were. He said, 'I'm sitting with you and Chester.' He told us that he would rather sit with his family than up on the stage with his teammates. No one bothered him. They let him sit where he wanted to. Dad was happy.

"The food was delicious, but I noticed that my father was not eating. He told me that he did not feel well but tried to disguise his feelings so no one would notice. It was then that I realized something was wrong. A month later, in August, I found out about his illness after surgery. He had a hole the size of a donut that had perforated his stomach for five years, but he had endured the pain due to his baseball conditioning.

"After hugging and saying goodbye to everyone and thanking

them and Tom Stultz for a fantastic time, we drove to the airport and took the same planes back home to Detroit. In the airport in Cincinnati, Joe Lapointe sat next to Dad and interviewed him. He asked Dad, 'Who is your favorite player?' Dad immediately said, 'Oscar Charleston,' a Negro Leagues ballplayer and manager. Joe and Dad laughed and talked for hours. Joe made Dad feel at ease. Joe is a remarkable sportswriter and a genuine person. He was a blessing to Dad and our family, and he continues to carry on Dad's legacy.

"Chester said he was utterly amazed to be in the presence of these history-making men, to hear their stories and to obtain their autographs. He was so glad that he had been afforded this opportunity and thought my father was an amazing man and ballplayer. Dad thought Chester was an amazing man, too, and was happy to have him along on this trip. I agree. This was a magical time for all of us. I only wish that my mom and my sister had been able to join us. However, because Dad had not informed us about the invitation in a timely fashion, they were not able to come."

When Dad, my sister and Chester returned home, Mom and I were anxious to hear about their adventure. I wanted to hear it all. I could tell from the smiles on their faces that they had had a good time. Man! I should have been there. Now I have to let bygones be bygones. I reveled in the fact that Dad was able to see his old teammates once again. This was significant because, little did we know, this would be the last opportunity Dad would have to see his teammates.

A few weeks later, John Collier and Joe Lapointe, sports journalists for the *Detroit Free Press*, came to our home to interview Dad. Part of the interview was done at our home on Carter, and the other part was done at Tiger Stadium, located on Michigan and Trumbull. (Tiger Stadium was demolished on September 21, 2009, and is now "The Corner Ballpark presented by Adient.") Pictures were taken by John Collier. Three of my favorite pictures that have been taken include a headshot of Dad and my son, another one showing Dad with my son sitting on his lap, and another with Dad positioned in a batting stance at the old Tiger Stadium. He was dressed in one of the outfits that he wore at the reunion in Kentucky.

Fans Called Him "Turkey," I Called Him Dad

In the first picture, of Dad and my son, they appear to be in deep thought.

In the second picture, Dad and my son have on baseball caps and baseball gloves. My son is holding a baseball in his hand and is poised as if he's going to throw the baseball.

Dad in one of his Kentucky reunion outfits finally standing at bat at Tiger Stadium, 1979 (*Detroit Free Press* photo by John Collier).

From the smiles on their faces, it appears as if they were having a good time. Most people looking at this picture mistakenly think that I am the kid in the picture. I continually have to tell people that they are wrong. The kid in the picture is not me. That's my son.

In the third picture, Dad had a baseball bat gripped in his hands and was positioned as if he were about to swing the bat. I've been asked by several journalists and a few others, "Why do you think your dad had a smile on his face?" My response always is "I think he was smiling because he was happy that he finally got a chance to swing his bat at Tiger Stadium."

Every time I look at that picture, I can't help but feel that I hit the nail on the head. I wish Dad were here to verify. I would love to hear his answer.

Dad passed a few weeks after the interview.

XI

A Great Soul
Goes to Rest

One morning in 1979, my mother got a call from her brother Paschal (we call him Uncle Pat) to tell her that their mother (my grandmother) had had a heart attack. At the time, my grandmother was in her 90s, and her health was failing. She was overweight, living alone and having difficulty getting around. During the conversation, Pat said they needed help taking care of her. He and his family were working and couldn't give her the kind of care that she needed. Hearing this, Mom decided that she should go stay with her mother for a few months to take care of her and to get things in order. Then she told me and my sister that she would like to take her grandchildren with her. She thought this would be a good time for them to get to know their great-grandmother and to see what it was like living in Birmingham, Alabama, so we said okay.

My sister took her kids home to get them packed for the trip. I called my ex-husband, James, and told him what was going on. I asked if he would let our son go with my mom to stay with my grandmother for a while. As expected, James' ornery butt said no. I told my mom that James wasn't going to let my son go and that she should just take the other children and leave. They left by train the next day for Birmingham. My mother stayed there for two months with three of her four grandchildren.

When they came back home to Detroit, my niece, Karen, looked at Dad and said to me, "Auntie, Granddad looks like he has lost some weight." I said, "Yes, he does, but I know that he has been eating

94

Dad's grandchildren in their Easter outfits, 1978. From left: Gary Stearnes, my son Tony, Karen Stearnes and Cary Stearnes.

because I've been cooking. When I don't cook, I get takeout. I think it's probably just because he's getting older." Karen was only 13 at the time. She looked worried, and so did my mom, so I told Karen, "Do this for me. Tomorrow, after I leave to go to work, watch Dad and see if he eats anything. Since you guys were gone, it was just Dad and me in the house. I'm not sure if he was eating or not. I thought he was, but I can't be sure. Most of the time, I just cooked enough food for the two of us. If he's not eating, let me know when I get home from work."

When I came home, Karen met me at the door and said, "Auntie, Granddad hasn't eaten anything all day." I went upstairs to find Dad. When I got to his room, I said, "Dad, you haven't been eating. I'm taking you to the hospital." He said, "Okay, Pretty Girl." My heart sank. I knew that something was really wrong because my dad never would have agreed to go to the hospital that quickly. He hated going to the doctor. We always had to drag him to his appointments, and then sometimes we still couldn't get him to go. He was stubborn about going to the doctor, even when he didn't feel well. Most of the time, he knew that my mother would come up with one of her home remedies and that would be all he needed. And most of the time, that worked.

Dad got up and walked down the stairs. Meanwhile, I called my boyfriend, Willie, who lived on the next block. I said, "Willie, we've got an emergency. Something is really wrong with Dad. We need to take him to the hospital." When Willie pulled into the driveway, Dad was sitting on the front porch, waiting for me. I grabbed him by the arm and said, "Come on, Dad, we're going to the hospital." We walked to the car, and I opened the back door. Dad got in, sat down in the back seat and didn't say a word. He leaned his head on the back of the seat and appeared really comfortable. All the way to the hospital, I was trying to figure out what was wrong with Dad. I was scared. I was hoping it wasn't something serious and Dad would be in and out quickly. When we got to the emergency room at Harper Hospital in Detroit, I wasn't prepared for what happened. I got out of the car, opened Dad's door and helped him out. We started walking towards the door. I told Willie, "Go park the car while I take Dad inside and get him signed in." By the time Willie found a parking spot, the paperwork had been completed and Dad was being admitted to the hospital.

A doctor examined him and decided to keep him overnight and to run some tests. My father was told to get undressed and was given a hospital gown. Then the hospital staff put him on a gurney and took him to an elevator. I stayed alongside my father. When the elevator came, the staff pushed my dad in the gurney onto the elevator and wouldn't make room for me. I heard the nurses saying that someone must not have been taking care of him because he was filthy and needed a bath. I heard them and responded, "My dad takes sponge baths. He sits in the tub in just enough water to cover his legs because he is afraid to fill the tub up with water. He won't let any of us stay in the bathroom while he's taking a bath, so if he looks dirty, that's why. Don't talk about my dad. Just do your job." I was furious. By this time, the elevator door had started to close and there wasn't enough room for me to get on. My dad tried to grab my hand, but a nurse got in the way. Dad looked at me, and I started crying because he looked like he was pleading for me to stay with him. I tried to keep the door from closing, but that didn't work. I pounded my fist hard against the elevator door and pleaded with the staff to please let me go with my dad, to no avail. I stepped back and watched the elevator stop on the third floor. I ran up the stairs. I looked in every room on the third floor until I found Dad. I stayed by his side until the doctor came.

Dad did not look good. His expression told me that he was in pain, but he never said anything. Soon the doctor came, closed the curtains around my dad's bed and checked him out. Then the doctor came from behind the curtains. The next thing I knew, Dad was being moved out of the room. I asked, "Where are you taking my dad?" A nurse said, "He has to have surgery, and we have to get him prepped." I found Willie and told him to call my mom and my sister to have them come to the hospital right away. I needed some help. I didn't know what to do, and I was getting more worried by the minute. By the time my sister and my mother got to the hospital, Dad was in surgery.

After the surgery, Dad was moved to intensive care. The diagnosis was a perforated ulcer. I knew this was not good. The nurse let us see Dad, and, while we were talking to him, he asked for "Cowboy." I left the hospital and drove to the stable where James was keeping our son. He refused to let Tony come with me. Rather than start a scene, I told James to bring Tony to the hospital. I said, "My dad's condition is not good. He's in intensive care and he's asking for Cowboy, so bring him!" Then I left.

I waited a few days and still no Cowboy. After the fourth day, I knew that they would be at the state fair horse show, where my son would be in a competition. I put a pistol on my hip, drove to the fair and went looking for my son. I was determined that Tony was going to see his grandfather before anything else happened. My father was asking for him every day, and his condition was getting increasingly worse. When I got to the fair, I went to the horse barns, looking for my son. I knew just about where he would be and discovered that he was competing in his Western horsemanship class. His class had just ended, and the winners were being announced. My son had won first place. I was so happy that for a moment I forgot why I was there.

Then, in an instant, I remembered. I ran down the steps from where I had been watching, walked up to James and told him, "Tony is coming with me to see Dad. His condition is worse, and he has been asking for Cowboy every day." James looked as though he wanted to say no; but when he looked down at my hand and saw it resting on the gun, that was just enough to get him to say okay. When the gate was opened to let Tony and the other riders out, my son was the last rider out. I grabbed the reins of his horse and told him, "Tony, get down. We're going to see Granddad. He's been asking for you." He immediately got down off his horse, handed his dad his prizes (a blue ribbon, a silver plate and an envelope with some money) and, with tears in his eyes, said, "Dad, I'm going to go see Granddad. I should have been gone." I took him by the hand, and we left.

When we got in the car, my son said, "Mah, what's wrong with Granddad? How come Dad wouldn't let me see him?" I said, "Honey, your dad is upset because I divorced him. Now he wants to punish me by not letting me see you. That's why he didn't let you go to Alabama with your cousins and your grandma. He didn't tell you that my dad was sick either, did he?" Tony said, "Mah, no. How long has Granddaddy been sick?" I said, "For almost a week, and he's been asking for you every day." Then my son cried. I felt like turning around and going back to give James a beat down, but I just had a strange feeling.

When we got to the hospital, I took the gun off my belt loop and put it into the glove compartment. I couldn't go into the hospital with a gun. To this day I don't know how I got away with it at the fair. It had to be divine intervention. We got out of the car and went into the hospital. When my son saw my dad, he said, "Mah, Granddad has his eyes closed. Is he asleep?" I got close to the bed, took a good look at Dad and realized that he was in a coma. I didn't know what to tell my son. I stood there for a moment, trying to decide what to do and trying not to show my son how I was feeling. That was one of the worst moments of my life, and I believe it was the same for my son. I told him the truth.

I said, "No, Son. Your granddad is in a coma, but he knows you're here. Do you know what that means?" My son cried and then said, "Can we go to the chapel and pray for Granddad?" I said, "Good idea." He held my hand. We found the chapel, knelt down on our knees and prayed. Then we went back to see Dad. After we left the hospital, I took my son back to the riding stable to be with his father. While he was getting out of the car, my son said, "Mah, will you come and get me tomorrow?" I said, "First, see if your father will take you. I'll be at work. Granddad might wake up if he hears you talking to him." Tony said, "Okay, I'll ask him." He climbed onto the front seat, gave me a hug, said goodbye and ran into the house.

The next day, when I came home from work, I hadn't heard from my son or James, so I assumed that everything was okay. Well, it wasn't. It was a Tuesday evening. On Tuesdays, I had to get ready for choir rehearsal. My plan was to go to rehearsal and then to see Dad, but first I had to get some music ready for the rehearsal. I asked some of my teenage neighbors from across the street to help me. While we were putting the music together, my next-door neighbor, Mrs. Brown, came over and just stood in my living room watching us. I didn't say anything at first because I thought she was just being nosy. Finally, I got irritated because she was just standing there and not saying anything. I said, "Mrs. Brown, is something wrong?" She said, "You don't know, do you?" I said, "Know what?" Now I was really irritated. I turned around, faced her with my hands on my hips and said indignantly for the second time, "Know what?" She said, "The hospital called me because they couldn't find your number or your sister's. They remembered your last name and your street and called me. Since I knew that you were at work, I went across the street and told your sister so I could help your sister tell your mom." I interrupted her because by now I was really pissed off and said, "Tell my mom what?" She said, "Your dad died this morning."

I was crushed. I fell to my knees on the floor and just cried. Everyone in the house tried to comfort me, but it didn't work. I stayed on my knees for I don't know how long. My neighbors just waited until I calmed down. When the tears stopped, I got up, walked out to the porch and sat down. After I had settled down, I went back inside and apologized to Mrs. Brown. By this time, my mom and my sister came walking through the door and told me everything that had happened. They hadn't called me at work because they didn't want me to be upset. They knew there was nothing that I could do. They would take care of everything that needed to be done while I was at work. That was the worst day of my life. I truly had lost my best friend. Dad died Tuesday, September 4, 1979, at the age of 78, three days before my birthday. My birthday will never be the same.

The next day, after word had gotten around the neighborhood about Dad's passing, one of Dad's buddies from the barber shop came to our house and told Mom that he knew Dad was gone because Dad spoke to him in a vision at the barber shop. He said, in the vision, Dad said, "Man, it's time for me to go. I'll see you later." Dad died that same morning. That was prophetic.

When Dad made his transition, at the following Tigers home game, sportscaster Ernie Harwell announced, "The Tigers have lost one of their best fans, Norman 'Turkey' Stearnes. May he rest in peace." We had no idea that he was going to do that. I will never forget it. It was truly an honor to have him make that announcement. Dad would have been so proud.

Joe Lapointe, then a journalist and now a family friend, called my mom to find out why he didn't see Dad at the Tigers' home game that Thursday, September 6. Mom told him the sad news. He said, "Sorry to hear that. If you don't mind, I'll do his obituary and put it in the *Detroit Free Press*." As a result of Joe's article, hundreds of people from the metro Detroit area and even from other states showed up at the funeral home to pay their respects to Dad.

Dad's funeral arrangements were entrusted to the James Cole Funeral Home on West Grand Boulevard in Detroit. A family hour was held on my birthday, Friday, September 7, from 7:00 to 9:00 p.m. We were amazed and very appreciative of the many people who showed up to honor my father. I remember thinking, "Wow! Dad had quite a following." I was overwhelmed.

Funeral services began at 11:00 a.m. the next day, Saturday,

XI. A Great Soul Goes to Rest

September 8, 1979, at Hope Lutheran Church on Chicago Boulevard in Detroit. In attendance were our immediate family, a host of relatives, friends, special guests and many people from the community and the surrounding Detroit metro area. The church was filled to capacity. Receiving all of this support helped my family through the grieving process.

The Brazeal Dennard Chorale, of which I am a member, was the guest choir. They opened the service with one of Dad's favorites, "Gimme Dat Ole Time Religion." When Mom, Joyce and I were making arrangements for the service, my sister and I decided that we should sing a song because we knew Dad would have wanted us to do that. Just before the liturgy, the two of us, along with one of our singing buddies, Chester Carter, sang "Goin' Up Yonder," a popular gospel song at the time and one of Dad's favorites. In case our emotions would prevent us from singing the song, the chorale was prepared to back us up. Thankfully, the three of us managed to complete it in our usual good fashion without a hitch. We felt Dad was with us.

After remarks by our longtime neighbor and friend the Rev. Welton Brown, the chorale sang "We Shall Walk Through the Valley." The Rev. James Howard, our special guest and friend, delivered the eulogy. During the recessional, the chorale sang "I Wanna Live So God Can Use Me," with Joseph Hatfield as the soloist. James Harris, Jr., a close friend and musician extraordinaire, was the organist and accompanist for the entire service.

When our family processed out of the church, I broke down in a torrent of tears. Something about walking behind Dad's casket made me realize that he had made his transition and that we would never see him as we had before. As the family made their way to the funeral cars, we shook hands, hugged and received condolences from people attending. The funeral home attendants put flags on the cars of everyone joining us for the procession to the cemetery.

The procession was longer than we had expected and a great tribute to Dad. As we made our way to Lincoln Memorial Park Cemetery in Clinton Township, I started to calm down. My uncle James McArthur comforted me, and I remember thinking, "Dad, you will be missed; and I will always love you." At the cemetery, we walked to Dad's final resting place. There we had a small ceremony where everyone said their goodbyes and the family returned to our home on Carter, where our neighbors had prepared a repast. The final cause of Dad's death, which was shown on the death certificate, was cardiac arrest caused by an infection that was a direct result of the perforated ulcer.

Many years later, after Dad had been inducted into the Baseball Hall of Fame, Mom got a call from Clinton Township Supervisor Bob Cannon. In the conversation that followed, he stated that he had heard that Dad was buried at Lincoln Memorial Park Cemetery. He said when people found out that a Hall of Famer was buried in their cemetery, they wanted to pay tribute to Dad but were having difficulty finding his grave. Mom said that was because the cemetery didn't allow above-the-ground markers. Dad's marker was a flat marker; and we had trouble finding it, too. Mom told Mr. Cannon exactly where he could find it. He said he already had that information from the cemetery staff. He added that there was a lot of interest being generated about Dad's grave and, because this was a first for their city, would Mom mind if he started a campaign to raise money to put a Hall of Fame marker on Dad's grave. Mom was elated and, of course, gave him permission to go ahead with the fundraiser.

The next step was to get permission from the National Baseball Hall of Fame and Museum to make a copy of Dad's plaque and to place it on Dad's grave. This marker would replace the hard-to-find flat marker already there. After permission was given, the Clinton Township supervisor set the campaign in motion. Once the word got out, donations came pouring in. More than enough money was raised in an exceptionally short amount of time. It took only *one day*! Mr. Cannon had to make a public announcement to tell people to stop. They had raised more than enough money. He was pleasantly surprised. So was our family.

What we didn't know then was that a lot of people like to visit the gravesites of Hall of Famers, whether in baseball or some other sport. Something else we didn't know was that to keep thieves from stealing

The first marker on Dad's grave at Lincoln Memorial Park Cemetery in Clinton Township, Michigan, September 8, 1979.

Family and friends at the Hall of Fame marker ceremony at Lincoln Memorial Park Cemetery, August 12, 2002. Back row, from left: Deontae Brown, Anthony Alexander, guest, Dan Dirks, Neil McArthur, Jim Petersen, Malcolm Thompson. Front row, from left: Augustus Hill (standing), Antonio Embry, Cary Travis, Vanessa Thompson, Karen Dye holding Kindle Dye, Mom, me, Joyce.

Family and friends at the Hall of Fame marker ceremony, August 12, 2002. Back row, from left: Anthony Alexander, guest, Dan Dirks, Neil McArthur, bystander. Front row, from left: Antonio Embry, Cary Travis (bent over), Vanessa Thompson, Malcolm Thompson, Karen Dye, me. Standing: Bob Cannon and Mom.

From left: Dan Dirks, Michael Ranville, Mom and Bob Cannon at the Hall of Fame marker ceremony, August 12, 2002.

the marker, it had to be cemented into the ground. What a marvelous and unexpected tribute that Hall of Fame marker is to Dad. I know he's resting in peace.

After the legalities for having the marker placed on Dad's grave had been completed, Mr. Cannon called Mom and discussed having a dedication ceremony for the marker. The invitations would be extended to our family and friends. Mom and Mr. Cannon agreed that it should be a celebratory event. We extended the invitation to our family members who lived in the Detroit metro area and a few close friends.

We were all excited and happy that Dad was being recognized in this manner. The ceremony was short and sweet, and the cemetery

Family and friends at the Hall of Fame marker ceremony, August 12, 2002. Back row, from left: Antonio Embry, Karen Dye, Malcolm Thompson, Jim Petersen, Vanessa Thompson holding Kindle Dye, Neil McArthur. Second row, from left: Anthony Alexander, Deontae Brown. First row: Cary Travis (frowning).

staff did a marvelous job cementing the marker on Dad's grave. Everyone was pleased and commented on how easy it would be now to find Dad's grave. This was also a first. There are no other Hall of Fame markers in that particular cemetery. Dad's is one of a kind.

The events leading up to the marker and the ceremony were very

Hall of Fame marker on Dad's grave at Lincoln Memorial Park Cemetery in Clinton Township, Michigan, August 12, 2002.

humbling experiences. I'm glad the younger members of our family were able to attend, knowing that this was something that they would remember for the rest of their lives. I was also happy that Mom was able to see the fruits of her Hall of Fame efforts finally coming to fruition. The smile on her face and the ensuing conversations she had about Dad showed that nothing she had done was in vain. Again, Dad, rest in peace.

XII

Daring to Make the Dream Come True

Getting Dad into the National Baseball Hall of Fame and Museum was a monumental task. After much deliberation and seeing that there was interest developing around the country about Dad, Mom decided that she should do whatever she could to make that happen. Diligently for 20 years Mom wrote letters to the Hall of Fame Committee, explaining why Dad should be one of the inductees. To assist in her efforts, a former Negro Leagues player and black baseball historian, Normal "Tweed" Webb, would send Mom copies of newspaper articles and documents from his private collection that he thought would support what she was trying to do. Mom would browse through the material and use the most significant portions in the letters that she wrote.

At one point, Mom received a letter from the Hall of Fame that said they were suspending inductions for an undetermined amount of time, and they highly suggested that there would be no reason for her to continue sending letters to them about Dad. When Mom told me this, I said, "Mom, don't pay any attention to what they are saying. There is no way that they are not going to continue inducting players into the Hall of Fame. They just want you to stop sending them letters. You're probably getting on their nerves, and they want you to stop bugging them. Keep sending the letters and watch what happens." Tweed Webb called and talked to Mom and told her basically the same thing. Everyone Mom talked to about this agreed that she should continue. The idea was that "the squeaky wheel gets the oil."

At the time that Mom started writing letters, something was going on to build momentum to get Dad into the Hall of Fame. I don't know if Mom's letters piqued that interest. Several sportswriters came to our house and wrote articles about Dad. One of them was Joe Lapointe. Another was an author, Richard Bak. He called Mom and indicated that, with her permission, he would like to come to our house and do an interview. Mom and I had never heard of this guy before. When he came to our house, I was at work. Mom said he came in, introduced himself and started the interview with Mom and himself sitting at the dining room table.

It was a typical interview. She said he asked a lot of questions, made comments and took several pictures. When I came home from work, I asked her how the interview went and she said, "Fine. He was a nice guy." Usually when someone would come to our house and do an interview, we would be contacted by the interviewer or see an article in the paper. What often happened, and still continues is, friends, coworkers or church people would approach me and say, "Hey, Roz, we saw you on television" or "Did you see that article in the paper about your dad?" and I would say, "No, where or when?" Then they would give the information, and I would check it out. For some reason, we're always the last to know. The communication has gotten better over the years, but there's still work that needs to be done. On occasion we still get surprised.

Several months after the Bak interview, I was getting ready for choir rehearsal for one of my singing groups, the Brazeal Dennard Chorale, when I got a phone call from one of the members, Khadejah Shelby. She said, "Rosilyn, I'm at the bookstore and there is a book out here about your dad. Did you know?" I thought she had to be kidding, so I said, "Know what?" She said, "I just told you. I'm looking at a book about your dad. As a matter of fact, there are a few of them." Now I knew she must be kidding, so I said, "Right, if you see some books about Dad, bring them to rehearsal and I'll pay you for them." She said, "Okay. See you in a little while." I didn't think to ask her about the book title because I thought she was kidding. When she got to rehearsal, I was sitting at the table and distributing music (I'm the librarian of the group). She walked up with six books in her arms, laid them on the table in front of me and said, "Pay up. These are all they had. If they had had more, I would have bought them." I was shocked. I looked at the books and saw that the title was *Turkey Stearnes and the Detroit Stars: The Negro Leagues in Detroit, 1919–1933* by Richard Bak.

Richard Bak was the same guy who had come to our house and had done the interview with Mom several months earlier. He did not tell Mom that he was writing a book. I opened one of the books and started browsing and saw Mom's picture. It was one of the pictures he had taken. She was sitting at our dining room table. I told Khadejah, "Oh my, I owe you an apology. I thought you were kidding. Where did you get these books?" She said, "At the bookstore on Greenfield and 10 Mile. That's one of my shops." I said, "What's the name of it so I can pass the word? Do they have any more?" She said, "No, this is all they had, but they are going to get more in." I didn't have to pay her then. She said I could pay later.

After rehearsal was over and I returned home, Mom was sitting in the living room, watching TV. I said, "Mom, I have a surprise for you. Look what Khadejah brought to rehearsal." Mom looked and said, "Where did you get these books?" Then I told her what had happened. When I finished, Mom was just as surprised as I was. She said Richard Bak hadn't told her that he was writing a book and that she hadn't given him permission to use her picture. We were flabbergasted. The book was published on January 1, 1995. Thankfully, as it turned out, it is still available in hardback and paperback. More than 800,000 copies have been sold.

Prelude to the Hall of Fame

Between 1971 and 1997, a combination of events took place to get Dad into the Baseball Hall of Fame. As a result of all of the painstaking and relentless efforts of Mom and several others over the years, the Baseball Hall of Fame's research department sent Dad a request to complete submission forms. In December 1971, the Hall of Fame obtained his submission form. Some of the people urging Dad's induction during the early years were Negro Leagues baseball player and Negro Leagues Baseball Museum director Buck O'Neil, journalists John Holway and Joe Lapointe, and "Tweed" Webb. Dad's friend and teammate Satchel Paige and others also contributed by repeatedly mentioning him as one of the game's best all-around players. It would be another 29 years before he finally was inducted into the Hall of Fame.

When I first posted my online profile on the Internet, I stated that I am the daughter of Norman "Turkey" Stearnes. Because there were sportswriters searching for Dad and his family, I thought that would be a good way to help people find us. One of the writers, Joe Lapointe, said he had difficulty finding Dad because he couldn't find anyone with the Stearnes name. I told him that was because my sister and I were married and were using our married names: Rosilyn Brown and Joyce Thompson. We have since corrected that. Now I use Rosilyn Stearnes-Brown, and Joyce uses Joyce Stearnes Thompson. Now we'll be easy to find.

One day in 1999, because of the comment I made about Bak's book in the customer review section, "I am Turkey Stearnes' oldest daughter," a guy named Dan Dirks sent me an email that said, "If you are really Turkey Stearnes' daughter, would you mind if we got your dad into the Hall of Fame?" Well, I thought he was being sarcastic because my mom had been trying for 20 years with no success. I responded (sarcastically), "Go ahead. Do what you can do. My mother has been trying for 20 years, so shoot your best shot." He emailed back, "Okay, I'll let you know what I need. I'll be in touch." When I got off the computer, I said to myself, "Yeah, right. Where did this guy come from?"

In the following weeks, Dan would email me and ask about our family's background. Everything that he did showed that he was profoundly serious. I felt so foolish. He also had recruited four other men who were working to get Dad into the Hall of Fame, and they were just as serious as he was. These men were on a mission. The men were Jim Curran, Michael Ranville, Negro Leagues and baseball researcher and statistician Dick Clark and Michigan State Senator Joe Young, Jr. They had read the book *Turkey Stearnes and the Detroit Stars: The Negro Leagues in Detroit, 1919–1933* and had seen a nationwide, mobile exhibit featuring Dad and the book when the exhibit had been here in Detroit. The exhibit was titled the "Negro Leagues Baseball Roving Exhibit." After they had seen the exhibit, read the book and had done some research on Dad, they were convinced that he should be in the Hall of Fame.

One day Mike called and said, "Rosilyn, I need a small bio on you, your sister and your mom, and I need it right away." I said, "No problem." I also apologized for the way I had responded when Dan and I had first met via the Internet. There is so much on the Internet that is questionable that I had thought Dan's first email was one of them. Boy, was I ever wrong! I sent Mike the bios, and he told me finding out that we were educators made things a little easier for him. He was totally impressed.

As time progressed, Dan and his crew went to work. Slowly but surely, I could see the progress they were making. Things were starting to look as if Dad had a chance to be inducted into the Baseball Hall of Fame. It was truly unbelievable. Here they were, five men that I had never seen who were so impressed with what they had read and seen about Dad that they were willing to help him get the recognition he so deserved. Mike called at least once a week to let me know what was going on and to get more information. We went back and forth for about a year, and then it happened. Working with Mike and his crew turned out to be a very enjoyable and educational experience. My family didn't know that it would take legislative help to get Dad into the Hall of Fame. There's a saying, "It's not what you know but who. The what helps, but the who makes it happen." Mike had a law office in Lansing right across the street from the capitol building, so he was quite familiar with the state senators and state representatives. Jim, Dan and Senator Joe Young were coworkers, friends and business associates of his. So was Dick Clark. Dick did the statistics for the book titled *Turkey Stearnes and the Detroit Stars: The Negro Leagues in Detroit, 1919–1933.*

On the day of the vote to determine if Dad would make it into the

Hall of Fame, Mike's wife called me and said, "Would you please talk to my husband? If your dad doesn't make it into the Hall of Fame, I think he'll have a heart attack." I told Mike, "Take it easy. If we don't get Dad into the Hall of Fame this time, we'll just keep trying until we do. Mom has been trying for 20 years, and this is the closest we have ever gotten in all that time. Don't stress. We'll just keep trying until we do. We're diehards." He said, "You won't be upset?" I said, "Of course not. I have enjoyed working with you guys. I really am sorry that I was being sarcastic at the beginning, but I thought, when Dan first contacted me, that he was just trying to get my goat. But when I saw the results of what your crew was doing and how serious you were about everything, I was sooo sorry." Mike laughed. He said Dan knew from the beginning by the tone of my voice that I was probably being apprehensive. He was a stranger, and if he had been in my position, he probably would have acted the same way.

The Dream Realized

The day of the vote was one of the best days of my life. It started when a news reporter from WXYZ-TV Channel 7 and a cameraman came to our house to interview me and my mom and to film our reaction to what turned out to be a successful vote for my dad. While waiting for the outcome, the reporter asked us questions like "Do you think he will make it? How will you feel if he doesn't? Will you continue to try and get him into the Hall of Fame? How will you feel if he does get in?" I let Mom answer the questions because I was too excited, and our phone was ringing off of the hook. There was a lot happening on our block. You could feel the tension in the air. All our neighbors were excited, and everyone was waiting in anticipation. The reporter was smiling, and the cameraman was filming every move we made. My mom and I were sitting on a couch in the living room by the window so that we could look at people passing by and wave. Everyone knew this was the big day.

Suddenly the reporter's phone rang. She answered, then said with a smile, "Well, what do you know? I think maybe you might have to try..." and then she paused. For a short while, she kept us in suspense. I put my arms around Mom and started to wonder. The reporter saw the looks on our faces and said, "Just kidding. I've got some good news. Your dad is now in the Baseball Hall of Fame. Congratulations! He made it." I hugged Mom, gave her a kiss and ran out of the front door and down the street yelling, "Hey, everybody, Dad made it. He's in the Hall of Fame."

I ran around the block letting my neighbors, and anyone else who was out there, know that Dad had made it into the Hall of Fame. The cameraman was running right behind me. When we finally got back to our house, the reporter was waiting to congratulate Mom and me. She let us know that we would be on the 6 o'clock news and asked, "How do you feel?" All I could say was "Great!" I was so overwhelmed and so happy for Mom and Dad that for once in my life I was truly speechless. There were no words to describe how I felt. My mom and I laughed and cried at the same time. It was a wonderful feeling. I just wish Dad had been with us.

Hall of Fame Weekend

The week of July 16, 2000, began a series of events culminating in Dad's induction ceremony at the National Baseball Hall of Fame and Museum in Cooperstown, New York. The actual ceremony was scheduled for 1:30 p.m. on Sunday, July 23, at the Clark Sports Center. George Grande was the master of ceremonies. There were five induct-ees: Sparky Anderson, Carlton Fisk, Tony Perez, Bid McPhee and Dad. Bid McPhee was a Major Leagues player in the late 1800s. Because he and Dad were being inducted posthumously, they were represented by family members. Mom represented Dad.

Our entire family received invitations to attend the ceremony along with information on planning for a successful trip. Arrange-ments were made for our family to stay at the Otesaga Resort Hotel, which was the only luxury hotel in Cooperstown. Our family members in attendance were Mom, Joyce and me; Joyce's husband, Malcolm Thompson; Joyce's daughter, Vanessa; my mom's sister Phyllis Wilson; Phyllis' sons, Kevin Wilson and Arthur Wilson; and Kevin's immediate family. Our guests who attended were Michael Ranville, Dan Dirks, Jim Curran, Dick Clark, Senator Joe Young, Jr., and a reporter from Detroit. All of us planned to be there for the weekend of Friday, July 21, through Sunday, July 23.

Cooperstown is a small, quaint town. Edward Clark came to Cooperstown prior to the Civil War. Because of his love for and increasing interest in the town, four generations of Clarks have continued to support the endeavors of the town. Stephen C. Clark, Sr., was instrumental in starting the National Baseball Hall of Fame and Museum. Currently, Jane Forbes Clark is chairman of the Board of Directors. There are no fast-food franchises in the town. Ms. Clark is determined to preserve the natural, genteel, picturesque beauty of the town.

Every year during induction weekend, the entire town caters to the inductees, their families and guests. Visitors come from all across the country to honor all of the inductees, past and present, of the Hall of Fame. All the activities for that weekend are centered on baseball and the inductees. Visitors also get a taste of the town's history, American history, art, architecture and beautiful landscape. More than 300,000 people show up every induction weekend.

When our family arrived at the airport, Mom, Malcolm, Joyce, Vanessa and I were recipients of their gracious hospitality. We saw people holding signs that said, "Otesaga Hotel." We didn't know it then, but in talking to the drivers, we learned that these were townspeople who had volunteered to be chauffeurs for the inductees and their families for the entire weekend. According to our drivers, the townspeople spend the weekend providing transportation and any other amenities needed by all the invited guests staying at the Otesaga Hotel. This included current and past inductees. We were impressed. I thought that was so cool. When we arrived at the hotel and checked in at the registration desk, we received our schedules for the weekend and went to our rooms to freshen up. Mom and I shared one room while Joyce, Malcolm and Vanessa shared another.

Security is very tight at the hotel and the surrounding area. Hotel staffers were posted at the entrance of the property, and credentials had to be worn and visible at all times. To prevent duplication, the credentials are changed every year. The drivers had credentials as well. One of the reporters from Detroit had told us that he would meet us at the hotel. We told him that, according to the information we had received in our packets before leaving Detroit, he would need to contact the Public Relations Department. We told him that if he didn't have the proper credentials, he would not be allowed on the grounds, let alone into the hotel. He said, "Don't worry. I'll see you there." Credentials were necessary for all events involving the inductees, the celebration at the museum and media opportunities. The reporter paid no heed to our warning. When he arrived at the gate without credentials, the gatekeeper would not let him in. He said that he was there to do a story on the Turkey Stearnes family, but that was not good enough. After trying to persuade the gatekeeper, to no avail, he was allowed to make a call.

He called me. I told him to stay at the gate while I would go down to the desk and see what it would take to get him entrance into the hotel. After I explained the situation, the desk clerk gave me a packet with the reporter's credentials so he would have access to the hotel and other media opportunities. When I handed him his packet, he said, "Sorry. You were right. This is so embarrassing. I thought my press card would be enough." Once in the hotel, he interviewed our family and our guests and then made his rounds. There were four other inductees and their families and inductees from previous years. He was off and running.

Excitement was in the air. This was a weekend I will never forget. We were treated like royalty. Everything was top of the line, and all expenses were paid. We paid only for incidentals and souvenirs. Breakfast and lunch were all-you-can-eat buffets with a wide variety of offerings, and dinners were gourmet. The rest of my family appeared to enjoy the gourmet food. Not me. I ate only a portion of the meals just to be polite and to please Mom. I'm not a gourmet person. I prefer home-cooked, soul food.

Friday was a free day spent doing interviews, taking pictures and basically getting familiar with our surroundings and other people. Mom and Sparky Anderson developed an attachment right away. Sparky was the longtime manager of the Detroit Tigers in the American League and the Cincinnati Reds in the National League. He had led both teams to World Series championships. He remembered Mom from an event that our family had attended at Comerica Park, and she was pleasantly surprised that he did. There were events scheduled only for the inductees and, if they were deceased, their representatives. At these events, Sparky graciously would come to get Mom and would be her escort for the rest of the night. You would have thought they were bosom buddies. On the schedule for the night was dinner and a welcoming party. When we first saw the schedule, we were worried that Mom wasn't going to enjoy herself. Sparky laid those fears to rest.

Mom and Sparky Anderson at the opening of Comerica Park in Detroit, Michigan, April 11, 2000.

Mom and Sparky had a great time. She was in good hands. The food was good, the music was great and Sparky Anderson was a character. It was an exhausting day.

Saturday started with breakfast and more interviews. On our way to the dining room, I spotted Michael Ranville, his crew and our other family members. I introduced Michael and his crew to the family. We agreed that after breakfast we should all meet and coordinate our schedules. All of us wanted to do some sightseeing to purchase souvenirs and gifts and to check out the town and the scheduled activities. There was a lot to do. Mom and Sparky hooked up, and we didn't see them again until just before dinner. Inductee-only activities took up most of the day for Mom.

Joyce, Malcolm, Vanessa and I were on our own. First on our list was the Hall of Fame store. When we got to the counter with our purchases, the salesclerk told us that we didn't have to buy anything because we would receive gift boxes from the Hall of Fame when we returned home. That was a pleasant surprise and saved us a lot of money. The items in the store were costly.

The next stop was the Hall of Fame Media Center. In this building my uncle Double Duty Radcliffe and other Negro Leagues ballplayers were signing autographs. When I saw Double Duty, I smiled and went around the table where he was sitting and put my arms around him. I said, "Remember me, your niece?" He said, "Oh, yeah!" I said kiddingly, "Yeah, you old goat. Turk's daughter." He laughed and said, "I know who you are, young thing. It's about time they put your dad into the Hall of Fame. They'll never put me in, but that's okay. I still get to sign autographs and to talk about your dad. We're related, you know." We hadn't seen each other in years and were making up for lost time. I stayed with Double Duty while Joyce, Malcolm and Vanessa went their own way. Double Duty never did get into the Hall of Fame, but he lived until the ripe old age of 103, passing on August 11, 2005.

After my reunion with Double Duty, I caught up with the rest of the family and we finished sightseeing and taking pictures.

After dinner, a special event for the five inductees and their immediate families was scheduled at the Hall of Fame and Museum.

Me and my uncle, "Double Duty" Radcliffe, while he signs autographs at the Hall of Fame weekend in Cooperstown, New York, 2000.

From left: Me, Vanessa Thompson (niece) and Joyce Thompson (sister) at Cooperstown, New York, 2000.

At the museum, we would be the first to see the exhibit and the permanent plaques of the inductees on display.

Saturday night was the gala affair. Little did we know about what to expect. When the time came to go to the museum, the five inductees and their families stood in front of the hotel and proceeded to get into their assigned cars. The cars were lined up in a specific order, and we were told which vehicle was ours. When the vehicles arrived at the museum, we were amazed at what we saw. There was a crowd of people cheering, and spotlights surrounded the area in front of the museum. Each car and its participants had their turn in the spotlight. It was just like being on the red carpet at the Oscars.

When it was our turn, we exited the car into the spotlight and the announcer said, "Introducing the family of Hall of Famer Norman 'Turkey' Stearnes. Onstage at tomorrow's induction ceremony will be his wife, Mrs. Nettie Mae Stearnes." We waved, and the crowd

Inside the HOF Museum, Cooperstown, New York, 2000. From left: Vanessa Thompson, Malcolm Thompson, Joyce Thompson, Mom, me, Buck O'Neil.

cheered. I felt like a movie star and thought, "Wow, if only Dad were here."

Once in the museum, we were given the grand tour and allowed to mingle with the others. Photographers and reporters were all over the place and took full advantage of the opportunity. We were pleased with Dad's plaque. It was a good likeness of Dad and one of the best we had seen.

After the tour, we were chauffeured back to the hotel. We went to our rooms thinking that we were done for the night, but Mom wanted to go over her speech. She was getting nervous. So we listened to her speech. That made Mom happy. If we hadn't listened, none of us would have gotten any sleep (especially me, because Mom and I were roommates).

Sunday, July 23, was the big day and what all of us had been looking forward to with great anticipation: Dad's induction ceremony. This was a day like no other, and it changed our lives forever. It was a hot summer day in Cooperstown, and we literally felt like dancing. Everyone was scurrying all over the place. My family and I were really excited about the events of the day. This whole weekend had an air of exhilaration, astonishment and disbelief. Now it was coming to fruition. Dad was getting the recognition that he deserved and carving out his page in history. It was truly miraculous but also a bittersweet moment. Dad should have been there. When I woke up that morning, I felt as though Dad were looking down on us and saying, "Well, Pretty Girl, better late than never." While Mom and I were getting dressed and chatting, I kept saying to myself, "Wish Dad were here to see this. Wow!"

We started the morning with the same routine as in the previous days, with breakfast, interviews and socializing. But the feeling was different. I kept thinking, "Dad is really going to be in the National Baseball Hall of Fame and Museum, and our family is a part of all this." I'm pretty sure that I can speak for my family, especially my mom, when I say that words could not describe how we felt. My family and our guests met in the dining room, and all of us were very animated.

Fans Called Him "Turkey," I Called Him Dad

After breakfast, we went to our rooms and changed clothes for the ride to the Clark Sports Center. Mom could not stop talking, and I could tell that she was a little nervous about giving her speech. Because there would be five speakers, Mom had been told to limit her speech to a maximum of five minutes. Mom wasn't happy about that because she likes to talk, but she planned for a five-minute speech. Mom had it down to a science. We can vouch for that because everyone had to listen to her speech and to time it before we came to Cooperstown.

According to the schedule, the ceremony would start promptly at 1:30 p.m. All attendees were directed to meet in the lobby to board the buses, starting at 12:30. Buses would make trips to and from the hotel until everyone was taken to the Sports Center. At the Sports Center, refreshments were being sold by the local high school. The ceremony was open to the public and free of charge. Approximately 50,000 fans gathered for the ceremony. Many were sitting on the lawn and surrounding grounds.

There were reserved seats for families and guests of the inductees. Our family and guests sat in the first three rows of seats to the right of the stage. We wanted to sit in the middle, but other guests had beaten us to the punch. Special seating on the stage was reserved for the inductees, past Hall of Famers and special guests, including the Hall of Fame Board of Directors. The inductees and their representatives were seated in the front row in this order: Sparky Anderson, Nettie Stearnes (Mom), Bid McPhee's representative, Tony Perez and Carlton Fisk. Mom and Sparky appeared to be having a good time conversing with each other. They were all smiles.

One of our guests, Dick Clark, statistician and a member of the Society for American Baseball Research, had arranged for a videographer to be there for our family. I realized, getting off the bus, that I had worn the right clothing. I had on a suit and a wide brimmed hat, which worked well because there was no shade on the grounds on this hot, sunny day. Most of the crowd had dressed in jerseys representing their favorite teams. The inductees' families and guests wore casual outfits more appropriate for the occasion.

Promptly at 1:30 p.m., Master of Ceremonies George Grande

XII. *Daring to Make the Dream Come True*

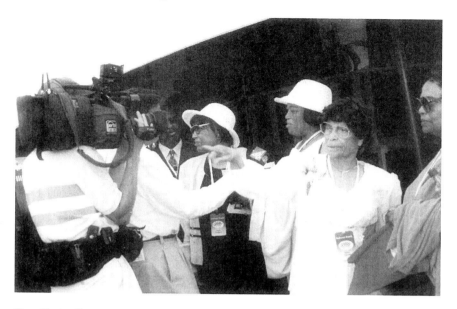

Family in Cooperstown New York, 2000. From left: Joyce Thompson (sister), me, Mom and Phyllis Wilson (aunt).

announced the start of the program. Everyone cheered. We were more than ready to get started. Mr. Grande introduced and recognized all the attendees on the stage. He gave a special introduction to the Board of Directors and Special Circle members of the Hall of Fame. Ms. Clark, chair of the board, welcomed the crowd with a short but attention-getting speech. Next was the moment we had all been waiting for, the inductees and their representatives. First to speak was Sparky Anderson. His speech lasted a little more than five minutes.

Next at the podium was the person our family had been waiting for, *Mom*. Our crew stood up and cheered. Mom smiled and began her speech. She spoke about Dad in a way that no one had ever heard before and with a lot of emotion.

"I am honored and happy to stand here and represent my family as the speaker for my husband, Norman 'Turkey' Stearnes, a star that was born to play baseball, one that belongs with stars. I prayed

Mom and Mr. Grande on the stage at the Hall of Fame induction ceremony in Cooperstown, New York, July 2000.

Mom giving her speech at the Hall of Fame induction ceremony in Cooperstown, New York, 2000.

daily for many years for this to happen, and now my prayers have been answered, and my patience has been rewarded.

"Turkey was a man of great stature. He was tall, dark and handsome, well dressed and very devoted. He was kind, quiet, honest, caring, strong, gifted and most of all loving. He had all the qualities that parents try to instill in their children. He never said an unkind word about anyone, and he loved baseball. We both did. It was his world, and he talked about it; he was one of the greatest baseball players to play the game. However, he wasn't concerned about being in the limelight, so the thought of giving an acceptance speech probably would not have appealed to him.

"We were destined to meet and were married in Detroit, Michigan. Born to us were two daughters, Rosilyn and Joyce. Both are professional singers. Rosilyn is a music teacher, while Joyce is a teacher of the deaf and hard of hearing. We have five grandchildren and nine great-grandchildren.

"After he retired from the Ford Motor Company in 1964, his daily routine consisted of waking up early, riding the bus downtown, taking long walks, and sitting in the barber shop [on Linwood] talking to his friends about baseball. He would ride the bus to Tiger Stadium and sit in the bleachers at all of the Detroit Tigers' home games. You could always tell when they were losing because he would arrive home early before the game was finished. Turkey and I spent many hours talking about the many home runs, triples, doubles and singles that he hit and how you couldn't play in the Negro Leagues if your batting average was below .300. He said that his power came from God and that his strength was in his arms and legs. He lived and breathed two things, baseball and his children, and he had a high batting average in both.

"I would like to thank all of the wonderful people who were responsible for my husband's induction:

The National Baseball Hall of Fame and Museum Veteran's
    Committee
Book authors John Holway and Richard Bak
Earl Wilson and the Baseball Assistance Team

Historians Normal 'Tweed' Webb of St. Louis and Dick Clark of
    Ypsilanti
The Ashton Museum of Kentucky
The Kansas City Museum
David Egner and the Charles H. Wright Museum of African
    American History
The African American Hall of Fame and Gallery
The Detroit City Council, Michigan State House of
    Representatives, and the Wayne and Oakland County Boards
    of Commissioners
Lobbyists Jim Curran and Mike Ranville
Dan Dirks, General Manager, SMART Bus System
Michigan State Senator Joe Young
Dale Petroskey and the staff of the National Baseball Hall of
    Fame
Joe Lapointe, *The New York Times*
All the sports writers from the following newspapers: the *Detroit
    News*, *Detroit Free Press*, *Oakland Press* and *Birmingham-
    Bloomfield Observer Eccentric*
The public-school districts of Detroit and Bloomfield Hills
The Golden Voice of Ernie Harwell

"Having my husband inducted into the Hall of Fame today will give our family some much needed closure. The months since the announcement have been chaotic and a constant reminder of how he was disrespected in life and, on occasion, still disrespected 21 years after his death. This is certainly an honor that he deserved, and we wish it could have happened during his lifetime so that he could have been a part of the celebrations and festivities that have been planned in his honor. Our hope is that the remaining worthy Negro Leaguers will receive this honor at some time in the near future as well.

"In closing, having the opportunity to be enshrined with Bid McPhee, Tony Perez, Carlton Fisk and Sparky Anderson is truly a great honor that my family is proud to accept. If you haven't been to Cooperstown, then I suggest that you add this place to your vacation list. It's a beautiful town with an awesome museum and many magnificent people, and the time spent here will always remain in our hearts."

Mom managed to stay within the five minutes allotted for her speech, and we were so proud of her. While she was returning to her seat, Sparky Anderson gave her a big hug and we all cheered.

Bid McPhee's representative spoke next and reminded the crowd that Bid had played in the late 1890s. This representative was the last remaining member of the McPhee family. He was elated to be a part of this celebration. Our family knew exactly how he felt. We were in tears. It was a sobering moment for us and the crowd.

Next was Tony Perez. His speech was short and to the point.

Last but not least was Carlton Fisk. He upset the crowd, in more ways than one, with a 45-minute speech. I could not believe how self-absorbed that man was. The more he talked, the more restless the crowd became, sweating in the hot sun. The enthusiasm of the crowd waned, and I had to contain myself. What had started out as an exhilarating and celebratory event was turning into a one-man appeal to his family. I wanted to snatch Carlton Fisk off the stage. I wasn't the only one. The crowd was getting agitated, too. When he finally stopped, the crowd stood up with a tumultuous roar as if to say what I was thinking, "Thank you, Jesus."

After the inductees and their representatives had spoken, the ceremony concluded. Then each inductee and his representative were escorted to a separate, chauffeured car for the return trip to the hotel. Family members and guests returned by bus. At the hotel, you could feel the excitement and the thrill of being part of a history-making event. As expected, the photographers and reporters were there to take pictures and to do interviews.

Our family went to our rooms and changed clothes. I decided to take a walk around town and to do some more sightseeing. One of the places I wanted to revisit was the Hall of Fame store and the museum. I wanted to get one last look at Dad's plaque and to take some pictures. While I was walking around the town, people recognized me as Turkey Stearnes' daughter and asked if they could have their picture taken with me. Of course, I said yes. I felt like a celebrity. In talking with some of these people, I found out that this weekend is an annual trip for them. Some of them have rooms in their homes dedicated to the Hall of Fame. They are true baseball enthusiasts. When I got to the museum, fans flocked around me and took pictures of me standing next to Dad's plaque. They were interested in hearing stories about Dad. I was happy to give them what they wanted. I always enjoy talking about Dad.

When I returned from the museum, photographers and reporters were waiting to take pictures of me and my family on the lawn in the back of the hotel near the water. The scenery was beautiful. Dinner was served on the patio for the inductees and their families so that we could take advantage of the view. The combination of the view, the camaraderie that we felt and everything that we had experienced the past weekend were all worth the trip. I can only imagine how Dad would have felt. These were unforgettable moments.

From left: Dick Clark, Mom and Nate Morris (cameraman) at the Otesaga Hotel in Cooperstown, New York, 2000.

XIII

The Legacy Bears Fruit

Turkey Stearnes Day at Comerica Park

Finding out that Dad was going to be inducted into the Baseball Hall of Fame was the beginning of some extraordinary events in our family's life. These began in the year 2000 and have continued since then. Our lives will never be the same.

The first of these occurred in the summer of 2000, when the same five men who were the main catalyst for Dad's induction didn't stop there. They convinced the staff at Comerica Park to designate a special day honoring my dad. They gave three reasons: (1) he was one of the best fans the Tigers have ever had (Ernie Harwell said that, too); (2) according to statistics, had it not been for the color of his skin, Dad would have qualified to play on the Tigers team; and (3) he had made Detroit his home until the day he died.

One of the five advocates, Michael Ranville, called one day and said, "Your family can expect a call from Comerica Park concerning having a day to honor your dad very shortly." When the call came, the Comerica Park staffer said the Tigers wanted to have "Turkey Stearnes Day" at Comerica Park on the same day as the induction ceremony at the Hall of Fame. She said that would be the only day available on the park's schedule. We responded that there was no way that would be possible. We weren't going to miss a once-in-a-lifetime event like the induction ceremony at Cooperstown to go to an event at Comerica Park. We thought, "Are they crazy? How could they even suggest something like that!" We absolutely were not going to miss Dad's induction ceremony and all of the activities surrounding it. I called

Mike about this, and he said he would take care of it. A few weeks later, Mom got another call from a Comerica Park staffer. I don't know what Mike said, but the staffer asked, "What day do you think would work for you?" This was a case of "it's not what you know but who." Mike and his crew were the who, and Dad was the what.

Turkey Stearnes Day at Comerica Park was one of the most exciting and fun days that my family has enjoyed there. We invited as many family members as we could in hopes that they would be able to attend. We have a large family. My mother was one of 12 siblings, and my dad was one of four. As it turned out, several of them wanted to come but couldn't for one reason or another.

The ceremony took place September 2, 2000, before the Tigers' baseball game that day. A number of dignitaries were in attendance and, as a special bonus, the first 10,000 fans were given a copy of the original portrait presented to my mom in honor of my dad. Artist Michael Z. Taylor drew the original portrait.

Mom, Joyce, myself and other members of our immediate family were escorted to the center of the field. There Mom was presented with several items. The first was a check for $10,000 donated to the Baseball Association Team (who confidentially helps baseball family members) in honor of Dad. Next was the original portrait of my dad, showing him in uniform in several positions during a game and in Sunday attire. Last but not least were a bouquet of roses and a plaque. The crowd cheered, and so did we. I said to myself, "I wish Dad were here."

After the presentations, I was escorted to the pitcher's mound to throw the first pitch. Before we came to the park, a staffer asked Mom who in the family would like to throw the first pitch. She called me, and I told her I would be happy to do it as the eldest of her two children. She said, "Okay, Roz." Mom and the rest of the family were escorted off the field to a suite in the upper level to watch the game with the rest of the family and approximately 40 of our guests. I made sure that the five advocates were among the guests. Another one of my guests was a 90-year-old woman who was a member of Mom's bridge club. She indicated that she had watched my dad play some of his games at Mack Park. She said that she and her family looked forward to going to see Dad play on Sundays at Mack Park. It was the highlight of their week. She was so thrilled to be invited that she arrived in a limousine.

When the time came to throw the first pitch, I was not alone. Another guy was standing next to me along with the Detroit Tigers catcher. While we were standing side by side, I found out that this other guy was going to throw the first pitch, too. I was thinking, "This is a new one on me." I had been to a lot of games and had seen only one person throw the first pitch. What was this all about? Then the guy turned towards me and said, "Are you as excited as I am about throwing the first pitch?" I said, "Yep." He said, "You're Turkey Stearnes' daughter, right?" I said, "Yes." Then he said, "You mind if I go first?" I said, "Go ahead."

The catcher told both of us that we didn't have to throw hard. All we had to do was get the ball across the plate as close to him as we could. We both said we could do that. The catcher got into position

Billboards at Comerica Park on Turkey Stearnes Day, September 2, 2000.

Me throwing the first pitch at Comerica Park on Turkey Stearnes Day, September 2, 2000.

Billboards at Comerica Park on "Turkey" Stearnes Day, September 2, 2000.

and waited for the other guy to throw the ball. He stepped on the pitcher's mound and threw it but didn't throw hard enough for it to reach the plate. The ball bounced a short distance from the mound and rolled the rest of the way to the plate. The crowd booed. As he was leaving the mound, he said, "You're going to embarrass me, aren't you?" I said with a smile, "Yep. I'm Turkey Stearnes' daughter." When I stepped onto the mound, the catcher said to me, "Don't do what that guy did." I said, "No problem." I threw the ball right to the catcher, and the crowd went wild. I did a little dance, high-fived the catcher and was escorted to the suite. Dad would have been so proud.

Negro Leagues Baseball Weekend at Comerica Park 2002

You may call it fate or luck, but I call it destiny. Events happen in life that let you know that there is a God who evens out the score. After Dad's induction into the Hall of Fame and Turkey Stearnes Day at Comerica Park, the administrative staff there decided to honor Negro Leagues ballplayers by having a special weekend in their honor. The annual Negro Leagues Weekend at Comerica Park began in 2002 to honor my dad and other Negro Leagues ballplayers. That first year, Ellen Hill Zeringue, vice president of marketing, arranged for our family and invited guests to enjoy the game and the festivities in a suite usually reserved for paying guests. She talked to Mom and my sister about the arrangements, and because she is a very personable professional, her conversations would include getting to know about our family history, not only as it applied to baseball but also our backgrounds and interests.

Knowing Ellen came with benefits. Not only would we be given a suite every year, but we would also be invited to attend the legacy luncheons, where we would be recognized as the daughters of Turkey Stearnes and we would be given tickets to distribute to family and friends for the entire weekend. Being a Hall of Fame family has its perks. When I think about our family enjoying the game from a suite, I wonder, "If Dad were alive, would he stay with us in the suite or would he still want to sit in the bleachers?" My answer to that would be "Yep, 'cause that's where the fun people are." And he would be right. That is still true today. I have a lot of fun in the bleachers, not as much so in the suite.

Because of previous conversations, Ellen knew that Joyce and I are professionally trained singers. My sister and I have been blessed with exceptional musical talent, which we inherited from Dad. When asked where we get our talent from, we say, "From Dad." Mom would always interject, "They got their musical talent from their father, but they got their brains from me." People always get a kick out of hearing her say that. Mom refused to be left out when we were being complimented. It's a family trait and one that we relish.

In 2008, on a Thursday evening, Mom and Joyce got a call from Ellen about a problem she was having getting someone to sing the National Anthem the next evening during Negro Leagues Weekend. Teena Marie, a famous pop singer, had to cancel at the last minute because she was sick. Ellen remembered that Joyce and I had said that we were singers. She apologized for asking at the last minute but asked if we would fill in for Teena Marie. My sister and Mom said, "Of course. We would be happy to do it, especially since this would be another tribute to Dad." Ellen breathed a sigh of relief and gave my sister the information we needed, which included being at the ballpark before the pregame show to have enough time to get ready to sing.

Joyce called me that same day and asked if I wouldn't mind singing the National Anthem that Friday night. I wholeheartedly agreed. This was totally unexpected, and I was overjoyed. Joyce and I were going to sing the National Anthem at Comerica Park in front of thousands of fans! We used to complain about some of the singers we heard and to say that we would do better if we had the chance. On occasion, Dad would hear us talking and would agree. Dad could have done better, too, but we don't think he would have wanted to sing in front of a large crowd. He was just happy singing at home and at the barber shop. Now we were being given the opportunity to prove that we could indeed do better.

Ellen sent her assistant, Elaine Lewis, to escort us onto the field at Comerica Park. It was a long walk from the suite to the field, but we enjoyed every bit of it. After we got onto the field, we were taken to a spot where we had to wait while the other on-field activities were taking place. We were told that we would sing after the first pitch was thrown. After that pitch, we were taken to our positions in front of the microphones and stood ready to sing. I was so busy thinking about Dad and what his reaction would have been that I didn't have time to be nervous.

The announcer said, "Singing the National Anthem will be the daughters of Hall of Famer Norman 'Turkey' Stearnes. Please stand." We were going to sing a duet a cappella. Joyce and I are members of a choral group, the Brazeal Dennard Chorale, which does a lot of a cappella singing, so singing a cappella wasn't going to be a problem. When

Singing the national anthem a cappella as a duet at Comerica Park during Negro Leagues Weekend, 2017. From left: Paul Fugate (interpreter), me and Joyce.

we started singing, the crowd started singing with us, but to our surprise, they stopped after a few bars. I looked at Joyce, and she looked at me. We both had puzzled looks on our faces because we didn't expect that kind of a reaction. As musicians, we knew that we had to keep singing, so we did. Near the end of the anthem, while we were still singing the last few words, the fans cheered really loud and gave us a standing ovation. On our way back to the suite, we received a lot of compliments.

Reshardd Harris (grandson) throwing the first pitch at Comerica Park during Negro Leagues Weekend, 2018.

Ellen told us, "We will definitely have to do this again. You guys are good." Since then, we have been singing the National Anthem during Negro Leagues Weekend every year. The year 2020 would have been our 12th year. I can see Dad now with a smile on his face, saying, "Those are my girls."

As an additional bonus, a member from our family is selected, well in advance of this weekend, to throw the first pitch. I was the first because I was the eldest of my dad's two daughters. The pitching has continued with the family selecting members in no particular order but the majority agreeing who should pitch next. Currently, the pitchers have proven that they have the ability to get the pitch across the plate and directly to the Tigers' catcher. Not only are they having fun but we look forward to the next weekend with great anticipation. We've done this for 12 years and we have a large family, so the question is "Who will be next?"

Commemorative Plaque Unveiling Ceremony 2007

The Detroit Public Schools (DPS) found my dad's induction into the Baseball Hall of Fame newsworthy. At the time, I was working as an accompanist for DPS and was assigned to the Area E Academy of Fine & Performing Arts East school located on McNichols and Annott in Detroit. DPS had a monthly newspaper, and I submitted enough information to pique the editor's interest about doing a story about Dad. DPS news editor Susan Watson invited my sister and my mom to come to the school to give their contributions to the story. Consequently, she wrote a story about our family and put it in the next edition of the newspaper *The Detroit Teacher*.

Several years after this story was published, an amazing thing happened. The students attending the summer program at my school got a chance to come to the unveiling of the plaque ceremony for my dad at Comerica Park, the Detroit Tigers' baseball stadium. The ceremony was held on Friday, July 20, 2007, at 11:00 a.m. When our family was contacted about the unveiling, I knew this would be a wonderful

Mom and me at *The Detroit Teacher* interview at my school, Area E Academy of Fine & Performing Arts East in Detroit, 2000.

opportunity for the students. Not only would they learn more about my dad, but this also would be a good history lesson for them. When I had first started working at the school, I had discovered that the kids knew nothing about the Negro Leagues, truly little or nothing about baseball and, more important, black history. I made it my mission to include this as a part of their education. I enjoyed every minute of it.

Ms. Kim Johnson, the head of the school's summer program, was a coworker and a friend. She already knew about Dad being inducted into the Hall of Fame. I told her that the plaque ceremony was free and that I wanted everyone at the school to be there. She was thrilled. I told Kim that the first my family had heard of the plaque was when a Detroit Tigers representative called my mom to invite the family to the unveiling. Kim was dumbfounded and so were we. None of us knew.

Dad's plaque on the side of Comerica Park at Gate C, 2007.

She said, "Wow! We are going to enjoy this. But we have a problem. How will we get the kids to Comerica Park? My program can't afford buses. They're too costly during the summer." I said, "Send permission slips home with the information. See how many parents would be willing to drive, and include the staff. On the slips, make sure the parents know that they are to meet at the school in case they need to carpool. Some parents may not be able to drive or don't have a car. If you don't have enough drivers, call me. I'll see what I can do. We don't want anyone to miss out. When they get to Comerica Park, Gate C, tell them to ask for me." We shook hands, and I left. I knew the kids would really enjoy it. This would be something they would never forget. They would have two constant reminders, me at the school and the plaque on the wall near Gate C. Seeing is believing.

Our summer program had about 50 kids. It all worked out, though. While everyone was milling around and enjoying the refreshments, the *Detroit Free Press* photographer came over to me and said,

Summer school teachers and students from Edward Duke Ellington Conservatory of Music & Art at the plaque ceremony, 2007 (photograph taken by Detroit Free Press).

"There are a lot of students outside the gate looking for you." I said, "Oh, wow, those are my kids from my school." He said, "What's the name of your school?" I said, "Edward Duke Ellington Conservatory of Music and Art. We're a pre-K through 8 performing arts school." Then I ran over to the gate where my school kids were, with the photographer in close pursuit, and welcomed them with open arms. I was so glad that they had made it. They were so excited. Some of the kids told me that if they hadn't gotten a ride, they were going to take the bus. They let me stand in the middle of the group, and we took lots of pictures. For once I didn't have to tell them to smile. They were all smiling.

In attendance were many of my family members, including my mom and my sister. Also, there were two ministers from the Southeast Michigan Synod of the Evangelical Lutheran Church in America, Pastor Patrick Gahagen and Pastor Skip Wachsmann. At 10:45 a.m., the Comerica staff directed everyone to find seats in front of the area where the plaque was located. It was a hot, sunny day, and the seats were hot, but we managed. The ceremony began promptly at 11:00 a.m. First on the program was the Greater Grace Temple choir. Then remarks were given by Tigers president, general manager and chief executive officer David Dombrowski; Detroit mayor Kwame Kilpatrick; Wayne County executive Robert Ficano; and my sister, Joyce Stearnes Thompson.

While the plaque was being unveiled, everyone stood up to get a good look at it. Joyce was up on the stage with the other speakers while the rest of our family was in the audience on the ground. My niece, Vanessa, was standing on my left and Mayor Kwame Kilpatrick on my right. Vanessa looked at me and said, "Auntie, don't say anything." She could tell by the look on my face that I wanted to say something. Despite her objection, I said, "That doesn't look like Daddy." Kwame had his baseball card of Dad in his hand, looked at it and said, "You're right. It doesn't look like your father." We climbed up on the stage to get a closer look, and all agreed that it didn't look like Dad. The plaque also had a grammatical error and statistical errors. One obvious error was that the word "complied" should have been "compiled." The plaque recited Dad's baseball statistics.

Family at the unveiling of the plaque ceremony, 2007. Back row, from left: Cary Stearnes, Dewone Dye, Deontae Brown, Reshardd Harris, Antonio Embry. Second row, from left: Anthony Alexander, me, Cary Travis, Joyce, Karen Dye, Vanessa Dye, Jimmy Dubose, Malcolm Thompson. First row: Kindle Dye, Mom.

Michigan State Representative Martha Scott (left) and me in front of Dad's plaque at Comerica Park at the unveiling ceremony, 2007.

NORMAN "TURKEY" STEARNES
1901-1979

ONE OF THE GREATEST POWER HITTERS IN BASEBALL HISTORY, STEARNES STARRED IN CENTER FIELD FOR THE DETROIT STARS FOR 10 YEARS (1923-31 AND 1937). A SUPERB FIELDER AND FAST BASERUNNER, STEARNES COMPILED A CAREER BATTING AVERAGE IN THE MID-.300's FROM 1923-41 DURING HIS MAJOR NEGRO LEAGUE CAREER. THE LEFT-HANDED SLUGGER WON SEVERAL HOME RUN TITLES AND WAS PERENNIALLY AMONG THE LEAGUE LEADERS IN HOMERS. IN THE INAUGURAL NEGRO LEAGUE EAST-WEST ALL-STAR GAME IN 1933, STEARNES BATTED LEADOFF AND PLAYED CENTER FIELD FOR THE WEST. HE ALSO PLAYED IN FOUR OTHER EAST-WEST CLASSICS. STEARNES WAS INDUCTED INTO THE NATIONAL BASEBALL HALL OF FAME IN COOPERSTOWN IN 2000.

NEGRO LEAGUE DETROIT STARS: 1920-31, 1933, 1937

FOUNDED IN 1919, THE DETROIT STARS BECAME A CHARTER MEMBER OF THE NEWLY FORMED NEGRO NATIONAL LEAGUE IN 1920, PLAYING FOR 12 SEASONS UNTIL THE LEAGUE DISSOLVED IN 1931 DURING THE GREAT DEPRESSION. THE STARS PLAYED AT MACK PARK ON DETROIT'S EAST SIDE FROM 1919-29 BEFORE MOVING TO THE NEW HAMTRAMCK STADIUM IN 1930. DETROIT STARS IN THE NATIONAL BASEBALL HALL OF FAME INCLUDE INFIELDER RAY DANDRIDGE, INDUCTED IN 1987, OUTFIELDERS PETE HILL AND CRISTOBAL TORRIENTE, AND PITCHER ANDY COOPER, INDUCTED IN 2006.

TWO OTHER TEAMS NAMED THE DETROIT STARS ALSO BRIEFLY REPRESENTED THE MOTOR CITY, ONE A CHARTER MEMBER OF THE SECOND NEGRO NATIONAL LEAGUE IN 1933, THE OTHER A CHARTER MEMBER OF THE NEGRO AMERICAN LEAGUE IN 1937.

Dad's revised plaque on the side of Comerica Park at Gate C, 2017.

Still, seeing a permanent plaque honoring Dad was a milestone. Words cannot describe how we felt. We took a lot of pictures with many people, especially the dignitaries, and thoroughly enjoyed the moment. My family had fun, too. After the ceremony, as an added bonus, the photographer sent me copies of all the pictures that he took. I shared them with the kids, and they loved it. That was another great day.

Jerry Malloy Conference in Detroit 2014

In 2014, our family was asked to give a presentation during the Jerry Malloy Negro Leagues Conference in Detroit. It was the 17th annual conference organized by the Society for American Baseball Research Negro Leagues Committee and the first time it was held in Detroit. The conference theme was "Turkey Stearnes and Black Baseball in Michigan." Larry Lester, chairman of the committee, called Mom, spoke with my sister, and told them to have our family prepare to respond to this question: "What was your fondest memory of Turkey Stearnes?" In preparing for the presentation, I was reminded of the lyrics "memories light the colors of my mind" in the song "The Way We Were," sung by Barbra Streisand.

At the conference, not only were we well prepared but also all of our responses were quite interesting and embodied Dad from a personal aspect. Our reflections about Dad were one of the highlights of the conference. Larry had told us that the main focus of the conference was about Dad and his personal life. The attendees knew his baseball story. They wanted to hear ours. Seven members of our family spoke at the conference: Mom, Joyce, myself; my son, Norman (Tony); and Joyce's children, Karen, Cary and Gary.

Karen spoke first and said, "Granddad would sit with us on the porch and make us play catch and tell us and show us how to throw and catch the ball." Mom was next. She said, "I couldn't pinpoint just one memory. I have a lot of them." Gary was all choked up and couldn't speak because my sister had just sung a song from the opera *Phantom of the Opera* as a tribute to Dad. It was a tearjerker.

Then came my turn. I said, "I have a lot of them as well, but one of my favorites is when Dad came to one of my softball games and saw me hit a home run. It went over the centerfielder's head. Dad told me later, 'Pretty Girl, you hit just like me.' After Dad told me that, my coaches told Dad at one of the practices, 'Mr. Stearnes, we don't know why you told her that, but since then we haven't been able to do anything with her. When we try to give her some advice, she says, 'My daddy said I hit like him, and that's what I'm going to keep doing.'" Later on, at home,

Dad grinned and said, "You do hit like me, and that's a good thing, but you also have to do what your coaches tell you to do. You'll help your team win a lot of games." I said, "All right, Dad. You should know." We hugged each other, and afterwards, I did what Dad told me to do. My coaches were happy campers.

My son, Tony, said his fondest memory was when Dad would walk through the house at midnight with a flashlight, checking all

From left: Me, my son Norman Brown, and my sister Joyce Stearnes Thompson at Comerica Park, May 18, 2012.

the windows and doors to make sure they were locked. Then he would go to each bedroom and shine a light in each person's face to see if they were okay. When he said this, the audience fell out laughing. We laughed, too, because everyone who had ever slept at our house knew what that felt like.

Last but not least to speak was Cary, my sister's oldest twin. He said that he remembered all the bus trips that he, his sister, Karen, his twin brother, Gary, and his cousin, Tony, took with Dad on weekdays. He said he would never forget those bus rides because they thoroughly enjoyed being with their grandfather.

The audience was impressed and gave us a standing ovation. Phil Dewey, one of the baseball researchers, said, "What great memories. Thanks so much for sharing."

Detroit Stars Centennial Conference 2019

Our family had another opportunity to carry on Dad's legacy when the Friends of Historic Hamtramck Stadium (FHHS) hosted the Centennial Detroit Stars Conference August 8–10, 2019, at the Marriott Detroit at Renaissance Center Hotel. My niece, Vanessa, was asked to give a presentation which she titled "Combining Forces: Restorative Options for Baseball Integration and the Inclusion of the Negro Leagues." Our family was invited to attend in recognition of Dad's stellar performance as a Detroit Star at this now-historic ballpark.

Journalist Ryan Whirty, in his article "The Negro Leagues Up Close," quoted Gary Gillette, founder and chair of the FHHS: "The primary organizing reason for the conference was the Stars' centennial, which no one else in Detroit seemed to be thinking about. A second reason was the general lack of knowledge about the history of the Negro Leagues in Detroit. This seemed like a good way to publicize the history of Black Baseball in Michigan as well as to seed the ground for more events next year during the national celebration of the centennial of the Negro National League in 2020." The conference covered the history of the Detroit Stars, the Page Fence

Giants, Black Baseball in Michigan, Hamtramck Stadium, other Negro Leagues topics and, of course, "Turkey" Stearnes.

The FHHS is a group of enthusiasts working to restore, preserve and promote Hamtramck Stadium because it is one of only five stadiums still standing in the country where the Negro Leaguers used to play, including Dad. The city officials in Hamtramck were not aware of the significance of this stadium until Gary and this organization got involved. Currently, the grounds have been renovated, and the baseball field is a thing of beauty. Now the organization is striving to raise approximately three million dollars to renovate the grandstand. I am confident that will happen. I have a tremendous amount of faith in Gary and his crew of supporters.

Along with two days of presentations, the Centennial Detroit Stars Conference included a bus tour that made stops at Hamtramck Stadium, the old Mack Park site, the Ossian Sweet House, the old Tiger Stadium site, the Motown Museum, the Detroit Historical Museum and the Comerica Park district. When the tour bus stopped at the Motown Museum, I talked to the DJ who was playing music and asked him to put on some hustle music so we could get the crowd dancing. He complied, and several of us from the bus and a crowd of other Motown tourists enjoyed doing a hustle titled "Wobble Wobble." That was a fun way to end the tour.

There was more to come at Historic Hamtramck Stadium. Because of their combined dedication and unrelenting efforts, Gary and his organization were able to obtain grants to renovate the field. On September 11, 2020, with the support of the Hamtramck City Council, led by Councilmember Ian Perrotta, the field was named after my dad. It will now be known as "Norman 'Turkey' Stearnes Field at Historic Hamtramck Stadium." Once the dilapidated grandstand is renovated, a statue of Dad will be placed at the stadium in his honor.

At the naming ceremony for the field on September 29, 2020, Gary declared, "The past is what brought us here, and the past is what makes this special." He added, "But what's gonna make this place come alive are the youth of today. We're doing this for the children of Hamtramck today and tomorrow and next year and the following year."

The coup de grace of all these events was the official announcement on Wednesday, December 16, 2020, when Rob Manfred, Jr., commissioner of Major League Baseball, announced that the statistics and records of the Negro Leagues will have Major League status. As a result, records from 1920 through 1948 will, after review, be included in the records of Major League Baseball. This marks a fitting conclusion to the centennial anniversary of the Negro Leagues. Dad and his teammates will now be known as Major League ballplayers.

As time goes by, there certainly will be more bittersweet moments, but my motto is and always will be "better late than never."

Epilogue

Dad put his all into everything that he did. He was an all-around great ballplayer and an all-around great husband, dad and granddad. What more could we have asked for? There are no words to describe just how amazing he was. One of the sad things is that he did not get recognized for his accomplishments until after he was gone. Why don't we give people their roses while they are still alive? Why do we wait until they are gone? I say it's never too late, but is that actually the truth? Or is that just my way of excusing the obvious? All of his life, Dad had to make lemonade out of lemons, and he did it with humility and grace. When I look back over the 33 years that I lived with Dad and recall how he overcame every obstacle thrown in his way, I am inspired.

It's mind-boggling to me that my sister and I didn't know we were in the midst of greatness while Dad was still alive. I think Mom knew because she tried unwaveringly for 20 years to get Dad into the Baseball Hall of Fame. They made a good team. She was his faithful partner for 33 years and lived long enough to see her vision for Dad come true before her own transition on December 4, 2014. Joyce and I knew that Dad was a great father and family man, but when we finally realized how great he was as a ballplayer, then the regrets set in. I personally regret not knowing sooner, not seeing Dad play and not recording the conversations that I had overheard between Dad and Satchel Paige. I would have been recording history. What an opportunity that would have been! Missing those opportunities still affects me. Fortunately, there were other people such as Gary Gillette and Joe Lapointe who knew and made things happen. Now the world will know, and the legacy of his greatness will continue.

Dad had a strong constitution. So did the rest of the Negro Leagues ballplayers. They played for the love of the game; and because of that love, they excelled. Dad played in countries that he never would have dreamed of, including Mexico and Cuba. He said, "We were treated better in other countries than we were in this country." Thankfully, with the integration of Jackie Robinson in 1947 into the Major Leagues, that has changed significantly for black ballplayers. Dad and his fellow Negro Leagues ballplayers were the forerunners. I can only imagine the impact Dad would have had if he had been allowed to play Major League baseball. The late statistician and SABR member Dick Clark said, "Stearnes was the greatest black ballplayer in Detroit baseball history. Not Major League or Detroit Tigers history, but baseball history."

The statistics of Negro Leagues players are incomplete, but the statistics that have been compiled about Dad clearly show that he was an extraordinary player. When the researchers talk about Dad, they say he was a "five-tool player." This means that Dad could run, throw, field, hit for average and hit with power. What a combination! He could do it all. I like that term.

I have my own term for Dad. In describing his personal life, I say he was an "eight-tool guy." He had integrity, was faithful, disciplined, strong as a bull, self-confident, supportive, loving and intelligent. As we say in the hood, "He was all that and a bag of chips."

I learned a lot of lessons from Dad and still have a lot to learn. Dad's dreams took flight in spite of adversity. When I think about what he had to overcome to achieve success, it gives me hope for the future. Losing him while I was in my prime was exceedingly difficult. It's hard losing someone you love, especially a parent or a child. It's as if your world has come to a screeching halt, and there is no room for anything else. I was a daddy's girl, and when Dad died, my heart sank. I truly had lost my best friend.

I had some of the best time times of my life with Dad and will always cherish those memories. If I could turn back the hands of time,

I would. Many people ask my sister and me how we felt when we saw Dad play. Then I casually remind them that Dad retired from baseball before we were born. Over the years I have come to realize that most people have no clue about the Negro Leagues and especially about Dad. They ask because they don't know. Some of the looks we get are priceless.

After what I've heard and read about Dad and other Negro Leagues ballplayers, I have some questions of my own. Why weren't my sister and I born a few years earlier? Why weren't Negro Leagues games being recorded for the world to see? Why weren't these players given the accolades they deserved during their lifetimes? Why? Why? Why? My questions may never be answered, but let's just say, as I always do, "better late than never."

When I gave birth to my son, Tony, and when Joyce had her twin boys, Cary and Gary, Dad had a gleam in his eyes. He assumed that these boys—or at least one of them—would follow in his footsteps and become a professional baseball player. In Dad's day, male children followed in their fathers' footsteps. Well, it didn't quite work out that way in our family. It's not that they weren't exposed to baseball. Dad played baseball with them and served as their mentor. They played catch on the porch and in the backyard. They also watched my sister and me play softball and accompanied us to all of our games. Playing baseball was an integral part of our life. Dad also took his grandchildren to many of the Detroit Tigers' games. They sat in the bleachers with him and had a good time. We were and still are a baseball family.

However, our children's preferences are basketball and football. Before Dad passed away, he didn't see this coming. He would have been disappointed but not heartbroken. He still would have been as supportive of them as he was for his daughters. After all, they were his grandchildren, and his love for his family was only matched by his love for baseball.

One important lesson I learned about Dad and the way he lived his life is that you should find something to do that you really love and not let anything get in your way. As Nike says, "Just do it." Dad and his teammates did just that.

Epilogue

As I complete these memoirs about Dad, it is the centennial year of the Negro Leagues. My dad's baseball career spanned three decades from 1920 to 1945. His entire life of 78 years spanned nearly eight decades. My intent for these memoirs is to show that his greatness is only enhanced when you know about the whole person, not just the baseball player.

My 33 years with Dad were the best a girl could have. I am and always will be a daddy's girl.

Appendix A:
Accomplishments and Awards

Among Dad's list of accomplishments:

- He was a home run hitter with getaway speed, which is where he got his nickname, "Turkey."
- He had an awkward stance at bat but could hit anything that came across home plate.
- He won the majority, if not all, of the races run between the players before the games.
- He won three unofficial home run titles: 1931, 1935, and 1939.
- He hit the longest home run ever seen in Cuba (more than 500 feet).
- He was one of the best centerfielders in the game.
- In 22 official at-bats, he had 16 hits for a .727 average.
- He was the best leadoff man in baseball history.
- He retired from baseball in 1945.
- He had two daughters, five grandchildren, 11 great-grandchildren, and 13 great-great-grandchildren.

Halls of Fame

- November 7, 1987, Afro-American Sports Hall of Fame, Detroit, Michigan
- July 23, 2000, National Baseball Hall of Fame and Museum Cooperstown, New York

---

Appendix A: Accomplishments and Awards

- 2007 Michigan Sports Hall of Fame
- Royals Hall of Fame, Kauffman Stadium in Kansas City, MO spearheaded by Baseball Historian Larry Lester
- February 19, 2010, Tennessee Sports Hall of Fame

Honors

- July 2, 1979, Commissioned as a Kentucky Colonel on the 188th year of the Commonwealth
- 2000, *Sports Illustrated* 50 Greatest Sports Figures by State, 28th in Tennessee
- 2001, *USA Today Baseball Weekly*'s Top 100, 25th place

Mom and the plaque at the Michigan Sports Hall of Fame, in 2007.

Appendix B:
Current Statistics
Compiled by Gary Ashwill

Appendix B: Current Statistics Compiled by Gary Ashwill

Batting Statistics

Player	YearID	Stint	TeamID	LgID	G	AB	H	2B	3B
Regular Season									
Stearnes, Turkey	1923	1	Detroit Stars I	Negro National League I	69	279	101	18	14
Stearnes, Turkey	1924	1	Detroit Stars I	Negro National League I	61	248	84	9	12
Stearnes, Turkey	1925	1	Detroit Stars I	Negro National League I	94	367	136	24	14
Stearnes, Turkey	1926	1	Detroit Stars I	Negro National League I	93	342	131	33	9
Stearnes, Turkey	1927	1	Detroit Stars I	Negro National League I	91	340	119	25	12
Stearnes, Turkey	1928	1	Detroit Stars I	Negro National League I	80	315	101	16	7
Stearnes, Turkey	1929	1	Detroit Stars I	Negro National League I	68	259	101	17	4
Stearnes, Turkey	1930	1	New York Lincoln Giants	Independent	19	73	31	9	4
Stearnes, Turkey	1930	2	Detroit Stars I	Negro National League I	35	129	42	9	8
Stearnes, Turkey	1931	1	Detroit Stars I	Negro National League I	38	133	50	10	0
Stearnes, Turkey	1931	2	Kansas City Monarchs	Independent	16	57	7	2	2
Stearnes, Turkey	1932	1	Chicago American Giants	Negro Southern League	44	168	49	9	2
Stearnes, Turkey	1933	1	Chicago American Giants	Negro National League II	41	175	62	12	5
Stearnes, Turkey	1934	1	Chicago American Giants	Negro National League II	39	154	53	7	7
Stearnes, Turkey	1935	1	Chicago American Giants	Negro National League II	47	170	66	10	6
Stearnes, Turkey	1936	1	Philadelphia Stars	Negro National League II	52	210	74	8	5
Stearnes, Turkey	1937	1	Detroit Stars II	Negro American League	18	64	25	3	1
Stearnes, Turkey	1937	2	Chicago American Giants	Negro American League	4	14	4	1	0

HR	R	RBI	BB	SO	HBP	SF	SH	SB	CS	GIDP	IBB	TB	AVE	OBA	SLG
17	70	85	17		1		2	2				198	0.362	0.401	0.710
9	57	44	17		2		6	2				144	0.339	0.386	0.581
19	93	126	45				3	11				245	0.371	0.439	0.668
21	94	103	41		6		11	21				245	0.383	0.458	0.716
19	79	114	46		1		5	13				225	0.350	0.429	0.662
24	80	78	29		5		5	5				203	0.321	0.387	0.644
16	64	91	38		0		7	12				174	0.390	0.468	0.672
6	31	33	12		0		3	7				66	0.425	0.506	0.904
2	26	38	14		0		3	6				73	0.326	0.392	0.566
8	29	33	20		2		1	6				84	0.376	0.465	0.632
0	6	7	2		1		0	2				13	0.123	0.167	0.228
4	43	25	21		1		4	11				74	0.292	0.374	0.440
7	46	30	18		1		3	1				105	0.354	0.418	0.600
6	42	28	14		1		2	6				92	0.344	0.402	0.597
6	43	52	23		3		5	9				106	0.388	0.469	0.624
10	45	43	19		2		3	1				122	0.352	0.411	0.581
4	16	18	9		0		1	1				42	0.391	0.466	0.656
1	2	2	1		2		1	0				8	0.286	0.412	0.571

Appendix B: Current Statistics Compiled by Gary Ashwill

Player	YearID	Stint	TeamID	LgID	G	AB	H	2B	3B
Stearnes, Turkey	1938	1	Chicago American Giants	Negro American League	19	69	18	2	1
Stearnes, Turkey	1938	2	Kansas City Monarchs	Negro American League	13	51	13	2	3
Stearnes, Turkey	1939	1	Kansas City Monarchs	Negro American League	49	185	61	9	1
Stearnes, Turkey	1940	1	Kansas City Monarchs	Negro American League	29	99	26	3	1
Regular Season Totals					1019	3901	1354	238	118

Player	YearID	Stint	TeamID	LgID	G	AB	H	2B	3B
Playoff Games									
Stearnes, Turkey	1930	3	Detroit Stars I	NNL Championship Series	7	30	14	4	1
Stearnes, Turkey	1932	2	Chicago American Giants	NSL Championship Series	2	10	7	0	1
Stearnes, Turkey	1934	2	Chicago American Giants	NNL Championship Series	6	24	11	1	1
Stearnes, Turkey	1937	3	Chicago American Giants	NAL Championship Series	4	19	5	1	0
Stearnes, Turkey	1939	2	Kansas City Monarchs	NAL Championship Series	5	13	3	1	0
Playoff Totals					24	96	40	7	3

Player	YearID	Stint	TeamID	LgID	G	AB	H	2B	3B
All-Star Games									
Stearnes, Turkey	1933	2	West All-Stars	East-West All-Star Game	1	5	2	1	0
Stearnes, Turkey	1934	3	West All-Stars	East-West All-Star Game	1	4	0	0	0
Stearnes, Turkey	1935	2	West All-Stars	East-West All-Star Game	1	3	1	0	0
Stearnes, Turkey	1937	4	West All-Stars	East-West All-Star Game	1	4	0	0	0

HR	R	RBI	BB	SO	HBP	SF	SH	SB	CS	GIDP	IBB	TB	AVE	OBA	SLG
2	14	10	7		1		0	5				28	0.261	0.338	0.406
0	6	13	3		0		2	2				21	0.255	0.296	0.412
7	42	39	17				3	12				93	0.330	0.386	0.503
4	15	25	16				0	3				43	0.263	0.365	0.434
192	943	1037	429		29		70	138				2404	0.347	0.416	0.616

HR	R	RBI	BB	SO	HBP	SF	SH	SB	CS	GIDP	IBB	TB	AVE	OBA	SLG
3	9	11	1		0		0	1				29	0.467	0.484	0.967
2	6	5	0		0		0	0				15	0.700	0.700	1.500
1	4	4	0		1		0	4				17	0.458	0.480	0.708
0	2	1	1		0		0	0				6	0.263	0.300	0.316
1	3	5	3				2	0				7	0.231	0.375	0.538
7	24	26	5		1		2	5				74	0.417	0.451	0.771

HR	R	RBI	BB	SO	HBP	SF	SH	SB	CS	GIDP	IBB	TB	AVE	OBA	SLG
0	1	1	0	1	0	0	0	0	1	0	0	3	0.400	0.400	0.600
0	0	0	0	2	0	0	0	0	0	0	0	0	0.000	0.000	0.000
0	0	0	0	0	0	0	0	0	0	0	0	1	0.333	0.333	0.333
0	0	0	0	2	0	0	0	0	0	0	0	0	0.000	0.000	0.000

Appendix B: Current Statistics Compiled by Gary Ashwill

Player	YearID	Stint	TeamID	LgID	G	AB	H	2B	3B
Stearnes, Turkey	1939	3	West All-Stars	East-West All-Star Game	1	3	1	0	0
All-Star Totals					**5**	**19**	**4**	**1**	**0**

Player	YearID	Stint	TeamID	LgID	G	AB	H	2B	3B
Vs. White Major Leaguers									
Stearnes, Turkey	1923	2	Detroit Stars I	Exhibitions Vs. White Major Leaguers	3	13	6	2	1
Stearnes, Turkey	1931	3	Kansas City Monarchs	Exhibitions Vs. White Major Leaguers	1	3	0	0	0
Vs. White Major Leaguers Totals					**4**	**16**	**6**	**2**	**1**

Fielding Statistics

PlayerID	YearID	Stint	TeamID	LgID
Regular Season				
Stearnes, Turkey	1923	1	Detroit Stars I	Negro National League I
Stearnes, Turkey	1923	1	Detroit Stars I	Negro National League I
Stearnes, Turkey	1923	1	Detroit Stars I	Negro National League I
Stearnes, Turkey	1924	1	Detroit Stars I	Negro National League I
Stearnes, Turkey	1925	1	Detroit Stars I	Negro National League I
Stearnes, Turkey	1925	1	Detroit Stars I	Negro National League I
Stearnes, Turkey	1926	1	Detroit Stars I	Negro National League I
Stearnes, Turkey	1926	1	Detroit Stars I	Negro National League I
Stearnes, Turkey	1926	1	Detroit Stars I	Negro National League I
Stearnes, Turkey	1926	1	Detroit Stars I	Negro National League I
Stearnes, Turkey	1926	1	Detroit Stars I	Negro National League I
Stearnes, Turkey	1927	1	Detroit Stars I	Negro National League I
Stearnes, Turkey	1928	1	Detroit Stars I	Negro National League I
Stearnes, Turkey	1928	1	Detroit Stars I	Negro National League I
Stearnes, Turkey	1929	1	Detroit Stars I	Negro National League I
Stearnes, Turkey	1930	1	New York Lincoln Giants	Independent
Stearnes, Turkey	1930	1	New York Lincoln Giants	Independent
Stearnes, Turkey	1930	2	Detroit Stars I	Negro National League I
Stearnes, Turkey	1931	1	Detroit Stars I	Negro National League I
Stearnes, Turkey	1931	1	Detroit Stars I	Negro National League I

Appendix B: Current Statistics Compiled by Gary Ashwill

HR	R	RBI	BB	SO	HBP	SF	SH	SB	CS	GIDP	IBB	TB	AVE	OBA	SLG
0	0	1	1	0	0	0	0	0	0	0	0	1	0.333	0.500	0.333
0	1	2	1	5	0	0	0	0	1	0	0	5	0.211	0.250	0.263

HR	R	RBI	BB	SO	HBP	SF	SH	SB	CS	GIDP	IBB	TB	AVE	OBA	SLG
1	4	4	0		0		0	0				13	0.462	0.462	1.000
0	0	0	0		0		0	0				0	0.000	0.000	0.000
1	4	4	0		0		0	0				13	0.375	0.375	0.813

POS	G	Def Innings	PO	A	E	DP	(PO+A)/9inn	FPCT
CF	69	589.7	136	2	5	1	2.11	0.965
P	1	7.0	2	3	0	0	6.43	1.000
RF	1	2.0	0	0	0	0	0.00	
CF	61	534.7	114	7	4	1	2.04	0.968
CF	94							
RF	1							
1B	1	7.0	8	1	0	0	11.57	1.000
3B	1	9.0	2	2	0	0	4.00	1.000
CF	89	761.3	195	18	9	7	2.52	0.959
LF	2	9.0	3	0	0	0	3.00	1.000
RF	2	14.0	3	0	0	0	1.93	1.000
CF	91							
CF	78	670.3	193	10	7	1	2.73	0.967
LF	2	13.0	2	0	0	0	1.38	1.000
CF	68							
CF	17	143.0	42	2	1	1	2.77	0.978
LF	2	18.0	2	0	0	0	1.00	1.000
CF	35							
1B	8	74.0	81	4	0	4	10.34	1.000
CF	30	245.0	72	4	7	2	2.79	0.916

Appendix B: Current Statistics Compiled by Gary Ashwill

PlayerID	YearID	Stint	TeamID	LgID
Stearnes, Turkey	1931	2	Kansas City Monarchs	Independent
Stearnes, Turkey	1932	1	Chicago American Giants	Negro Southern League
Stearnes, Turkey	1932	1	Chicago American Giants	Negro Southern League
Stearnes, Turkey	1933	1	Chicago American Giants	Negro National League II
Stearnes, Turkey	1933	1	Chicago American Giants	Negro National League II
Stearnes, Turkey	1934	1	Chicago American Giants	Negro National League II
Stearnes, Turkey	1935	1	Chicago American Giants	Negro National League II
Stearnes, Turkey	1935	1	Chicago American Giants	Negro National League II
Stearnes, Turkey	1936	1	Philadelphia Stars	Negro National League II
Stearnes, Turkey	1936	1	Philadelphia Stars	Negro National League II
Stearnes, Turkey	1937	1	Detroit Stars II	Negro American League
Stearnes, Turkey	1937	1	Detroit Stars II	Negro American League
Stearnes, Turkey	1937	2	Chicago American Giants	Negro American League
Stearnes, Turkey	1938	1	Chicago American Giants	Negro American League
Stearnes, Turkey	1938	2	Kansas City Monarchs	Negro American League
Stearnes, Turkey	1939	1	Kansas City Monarchs	Negro American League
Stearnes, Turkey	1940	1	Kansas City Monarchs	Negro American League

PlayerID	YearID	Stint	TeamID	LgID
Playoffs				
Stearnes, Turkey	1930	3	Detroit Stars I	NNL Championship Series
Stearnes, Turkey	1932	2	Chicago American Giants	NSL Championship Series
Stearnes, Turkey	1934	2	Chicago American Giants	NNL Championship Series
Stearnes, Turkey	1937	3	Chicago American Giants	NAL Championship Series
Stearnes, Turkey	1939	2	Kansas City Monarchs	NAL Championship Series

PlayerID	YearID	Stint	TeamID	LgID
All-Star Games				
Stearnes, Turkey	1933	2	West All-Stars	East-West All-Star Game
Stearnes, Turkey	1934	3	West All-Stars	East-West All-Star Game
Stearnes, Turkey	1935	2	West All-Stars	East-West All-Star Game
Stearnes, Turkey	1937	4	West All-Stars	East-West All-Star Game
Stearnes, Turkey	1939	3	West All-Stars	East-West All-Star Game

POS	G	Def Innings	PO	A	E	DP	(PO+A)/9inn	FPCT
CF	16	125.7	29	0	1	0	2.08	0.967
CF	43							
PR	1							
CF	41	344.7	86	4	5	0	2.35	0.947
LF	1	6.0	0	0	0	0	0.00	
CF	39	329.7	88	2	1	1	2.46	0.989
CF	46	382.3	86	3	5	1	2.10	0.947
PH	1							
CF	50	425.3	120	5	5	0	2.64	0.962
LF	3	22.0	4	0	0	0	1.64	1.000
CF	17	141.0	34	2	3	1	2.30	0.923
PH	1							
CF	4	35.0	11	0	0	0	2.83	1.000
CF	19	166.0	42	1	2	0	2.33	0.956
CF	13	106.0	16	1	1	0	1.44	0.944
CF	49							
CF	29							

POS	G	Def Innings	PO	A	E	DP	(PO+A)/9inn	FPCT
CF	7	61.0	11	1	3	0	1.77	0.800
CF	2	18.0	4	0	0	0	2.00	1.000
CF	6	51.0	9	0	0	0	1.59	1.000
CF	4	42.0	9	2	0	1	2.36	1.000
CF	5							

POS	G	Def Innings	PO	A	E	DP	(PO+A)/9inn	FPCT
CF	1	9.0	3	0	0	0	3.00	1.000
CF	1	9.0	1	0	0	0	1.00	1.000
RF	1	5.0	0	0	0	0	0.00	
CF	1	9.0	5	0	0	0	5.00	1.000
RF	1	8.0	2	0	0	0	2.25	1.000

Appendix B: Current Statistics Compiled by Gary Ashwill

PlayerID	YearID	Stint	TeamID	LgID
Vs. White Major Leaguers				
Stearnes, Turkey	1923	2	Detroit Stars I	Exhibition Games vs. White Major Leaguers
Stearnes, Turkey	1923	2	Detroit Stars I	Exhibition Games vs. White Major Leaguers
Stearnes, Turkey	1931	3	Kansas City Monarchs	Exhibition Games vs. White Major Leaguers

Pitching Statistics

PlayerID	YearID	Stint	TeamID	LgID	W	L	SV	G	GS	CG	SHO	IP
Stearnes, Turkey	1923	1	Detroit Stars	Negro National League I	0	1	0	1	1	0	0	7

POS	G	Def Innings	PO	A	E	DP	(PO+A)/9inn	FPCT
CF	1	9.0	4	0	0	0	4.00	1.000
LF	2	18.0	5	0	0	0	2.50	1.000
CF	1	9.0	0	0	0	0	0.00	

BFP	AB	H	D	T	HR	R	ER	BB	SO	HBP	SF	SH	SB	CS	DP	WP	BK	IBB	GF
37	31	13			3	14	12	4	2	1						0	0		0

Index

Index

Index

Page, Ted 89
Paige, Satchel 13–14, 84, 89, 110, 148
Pearl High School 11
Petersen, Jim 102, 104
plaques 138–142, 153
"Pretty Girl" 13, 20, 29, 36, 39, 42–43,
 50, 56, 72–73, 94, 120, 143

racial discrimination 5–6
Radcliffe, "Double Duty" 14–15, 17, 85,
 118–119
Rankin, Mr. and Mrs. 76–77
Ranville, Michael 111, 115, 118, 129
retirement 2, 3, 9, 16, 19, 49, 52, 82–83,
 85–86, 125, 151, 153
River Rouge Plant 18, 49
Robinson, Jackie 8, 150
Rogan, Bullet 13
Rosilyn 1–3, 9, 22–23, 58, 77, 90, 109,
 111–112, 125
royal family 1
Ruth 46–47

Scott, Martha 142
Smith, Mr. 51–52
Society for American Baseball Research
 (SABR) 1, 4, 24, 122, 150
Spanish Flu pandemic 6, 11
spelling bee 45
Stearnes, Cary 95, 142
Stearnes, Cary, Jr. 103–104, 142
Stearnes, Gary 95
Stearnes, Karen 95
Stearnes, Nettie 2, 122

Stearnes, Norman Thomas 1, 2, 4, 11–13,
 100, 111, 123, 135
Stephens, "Country" Jake 88
Stultz, Tom 88
Syrennia 46–47

Thomas, Clint 88–89
Thompson, Joyce Stearnes 1, 22, 111,
 141, 145
Thompson, Malcolm 104–105, 120, 142
Thompson, Vanessa 103–105, 119, 120
Tiger Stadium 9, 84, 91, 93, 125, 147
Tony 2, 70, 72, 74–75, 77–78, 80, 95,
 97–99, 1114, 122, 126–127, 144–146,
 151
Trouppe, Quincy 89
"Turkey" Stearnes Day at Comerica Park
 129–130, 131, 132–133

Uncle James 101

Wachsmann, Pastor Skip 141
Wayne State University 68
Webb, "Tweed" 4, 108
Wilson, Arthur 115
Wilson, Kevin 115
Wilson, Phyllis 115, 123
World War I 6
World War II 6

Young, Sen. Joe, Jr. 112, 115
Young, T.J. 13

Zeringue, Ellen 133